Inkle Weaving

by Helene Bress

The Macramé Book
(films:)
This Is Inkle Weaving
Macramé

INKLE WEAVING

Helene Bress

Photographs by Allen Bress
Drawings by Trudy Nicholson and Seymour Bress

Charles Scribner's Sons ———◆◎◆——— *New York*

Library of Congress Cataloging in Publication Data

Bress, Helene.
  Inkle weaving.
    1. Inkle weaving.   I. Title.
TT848.B72   746.1'4   74–8426
ISBN 0–684–13870–0

1 3 5 7 9 11 13 15 17 19 C/C 20 18 16 14 12 10 8 6 4 2

Printed in the United States of America

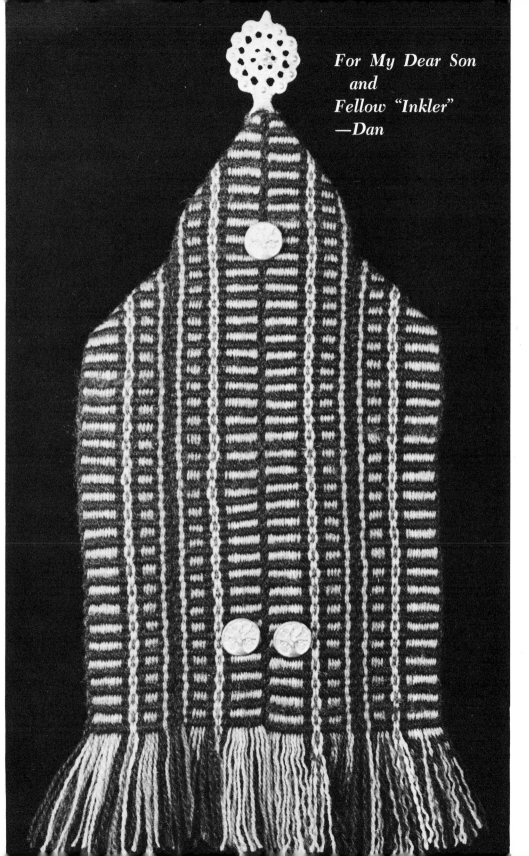

For My Dear Son
and
Fellow "Inkler"
—Dan

Acknowledgements

To receive an unusual skein of yarn in the mail from a friend, to have another immediately respond to an SOS call, and to receive an excited phone call from still another, saying, "Helene, I came across a quote I think you'll be interested in . . ."—all add to the rewarding—yet sometimes lonely—job of writing.

Thank you, Doramay Keasbey, for your interest, ideas, and the pick-up patterns you designed when time was running out on me. Thank you, Doris Bowman and Rita Adrosko, for sharing with me the bits of pertinent information that were available at the Smithsonian Institution in Washington, D.C.

To those who lent their pieces to be photographed and to those who lent their support in other important ways—thank you, too.

Each member of my family helped in his own way—

During school holidays, Dan undertook to weave several of the more intricate pieces in this book.

Allen was my very exacting, very competent, very easy to work with photographer.

Steven put in food for thought—and always helped to keep life in perspective by letting me know, "It's time to eat".

My liberated husband, Seymour, did a great number of the technical drawings, photographed when Allen was away at school, typed the manuscript, and did much of the unrewarding but necessary scut-work in compiling a book. Then, too, I'd ask, "What do you think of this idea?"—and he'd listen. . . .

A helpful hand when needed and no pressure in-between, characterized my easy to work with editor, Elinor Parker. Her secretary, April Ferris, was a friend in need.

Ever so easy to work with, reliable, and competent was Trudy Nicholson, who did the drawings as noted.

David Lunn, my book designer, very scrupulously "put it all together." And when I said, "Please, could this picture be a little larger?"—he tried to accommodate.

Thanks to all.

Contents

Inkle Weaving

INKLE LOOM

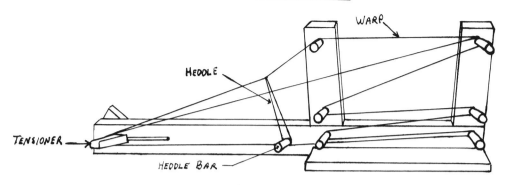

WARP

HEDDLE

TENSIONER

HEDDLE BAR

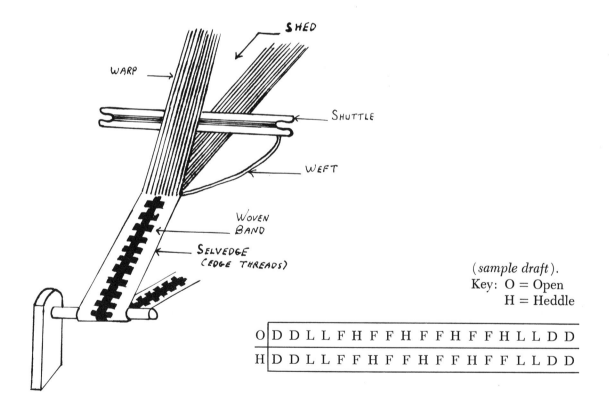

SHED

WARP

SHUTTLE

WEFT

WOVEN BAND

SELVEDGE (EDGE THREADS)

(sample draft).
Key: O = Open
H = Heddle

O	D	D	L	L	F	H	F	F	H	F	F	H	F	F	H	L	L	D	D
H	D	D	L	L	F	F	H	F	F	H	F	F	H	F	F	L	L	D	D

Introduction

*I*nkle weaving is one small facet of the whole world of weaving. I had thought that within a rather short time, I could thoroughly explore this field—and completely exhaust all possibilities within it. Not so! The more I explored, the more ideas I got for further exploration. As time ran on, I became disappointed and discouraged. I couldn't do what I set out to do. No, I couldn't—and after some reflection on the subject, I was glad. In weaving, there are always new worlds to conquer. That's what makes it so exciting. Inkle weaving is no exception.

Here is my introduction to inkle weaving. May you have a pleasant journey through this book—and go on to chart your own course—in your own way.

(*1*). Floor model inkle loom. Cherry wood. Designed and constructed by Seymour Bress.

(*2*). Below: Table model inkle loom. Manufactured by the Schacht Spindle Company.

I. *Get Yourself a LOOM*

Weaving on the inkle loom is fun! The loom itself is simply designed, portable, versatile, and easily constructed. Here are the two styles of looms I recommend most highly.

Most of the samples for this book were made on the floor loom that is pictured. I find it comfortable to work at and aesthetically pleasing. Since it is free standing, I just need to pull up a chair and start to weave. However, once I find a convenient place to position my table loom, I find *that* comfortable to work on, too. Take your choice!

(*3*). Close up of tensioning device on the Schacht loom. Although construction details differ among the open-sided inkle looms, their appearance is quite similar. Often, tension devices vary greatly between models. This tensioner works extremely well.

(4). ABOVE: Another style of table model inkle loom.

An inkle loom should:

be sturdily constructed

have a strong, easy to control tension device or tensioner

be easy to set up and warp

be comfortable to work at

Many other styles of inkle looms are available. The one in illustration 4 is quite acceptable.

(5). Close-up of tensioning device. This tensioner is quite adequate.

Despite Herculean efforts to remedy the situation, I have found that the tensioner on the loom in illustration 6 tends to bend after a while.

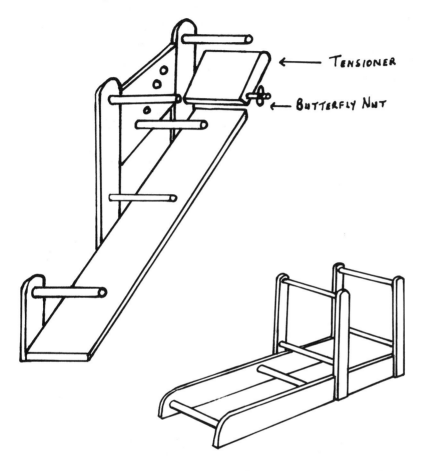

← TENSIONER

← BUTTERFLY NUT

(6). Table model inkle loom. Experience has shown that the tensioner on this style loom tends to bend out of shape.

(7). Two-sided inkle loom. Because this style is very tedious to warp, it is not recommended.

The two sided inkle loom (illustration 7) can nip the enthusiasm of the most energetic of people. It is very tedious to set up. It may appear that you can weave a wider fabric on a two-sided inkle loom. Well, you can put more threads on it, but weaving it will probably be quite difficult. You see, the inkle band is usually a warp-faced fabric—that is, the threads on the loom touch one another and form the pattern. Under most circumstances, it is difficult—and sometimes almost impossible—to weave a wide, warp-faced fabric.

7

The looms I have recommended are open on one side. This makes them very easy to set-up or warp. (See chart, page 2.)

As you weave, the threads on the loom (the warp threads), shorten. Without a tensioning device, the threads would get tighter and tighter, making further weaving difficult and sometimes impossible. Also, it would become too difficult to bring the unwoven warp threads forward as they are needed. Therefore, an inkle loom must have a strong, easy to control tensioning device.

To ready the loom for weaving, warp threads are strung from one dowel to the next. The warp threads will put the dowels under a considerable amount of pressure. For this reason, the frame should be very sturdily constructed and the dowels should be stout. A very minimum of five dowels are needed for these looms. The more dowels, the more convolutions the warp threads can make, and the longer the inkle band can be made.

Except for the tension peg, the dowels in the looms pictured are glued into place. You can put your warp threads around some of the dowels, or go back and forth around all of them. The floor loom can hold up to 124 inches (finished size about 105″) and the table model 110 inches (finished size about 94″). Less than this can be put on. (See section on warping.)

The exact position of the dowels is not critical. While sitting before the loom, you should be able to reach behind the heddles easily (see drawing, page 25). Your arm reach, then, determines the position of the heddle bar. For the average person, this will be about 14 inches. The heddle bar and the top bar should be about 7–9 inches apart so that the "open" warp threads can move up and down freely for a few inches.

The other dowels are placed randomly—yet thoughtfully. The warp threads will meander back and forth. When possible, there should be some space between layers of threads. Eventually, the threads must wander home to the front peg. The number of dowels needed is determined by the path your threads will follow. The looms pictured offer solid ideas about this, but other ways are possible and plausible. The looms that I've discussed, and the loom plans which follow, incorporate these important features.

LUMBER TO USE - Any hardwood such as
Birch, Maple, Oak, Cherry or Walnut

Scale - 1 square = 1"

Materials Needed

7 – Dowels – 3/4" x 6¼"
A – 3/4" x 14" x 4½"
B – 3/4" x 30" x 2½"
C – 1¼" x 9" x 2½"
D – 1¼" x 9" x 2½"
E – 3/4" x 5 3/4" x 1½"
1 – ¼" Hanger Bolt with washer and
    butterfly nut. The hanger
    bolt is screwed into "E".

4 – 1" x #9 wood screws for "C" & "D"
2 – 1½" #10 wood screws for "B"

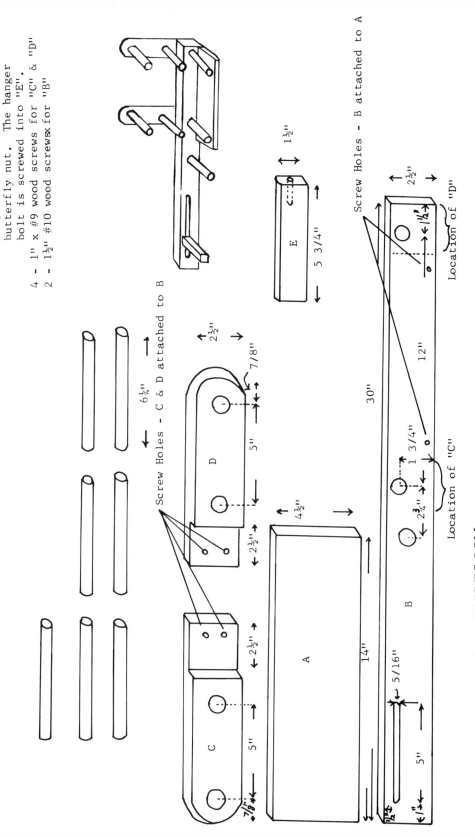

(8) Loom plans—TABLE LOOM.

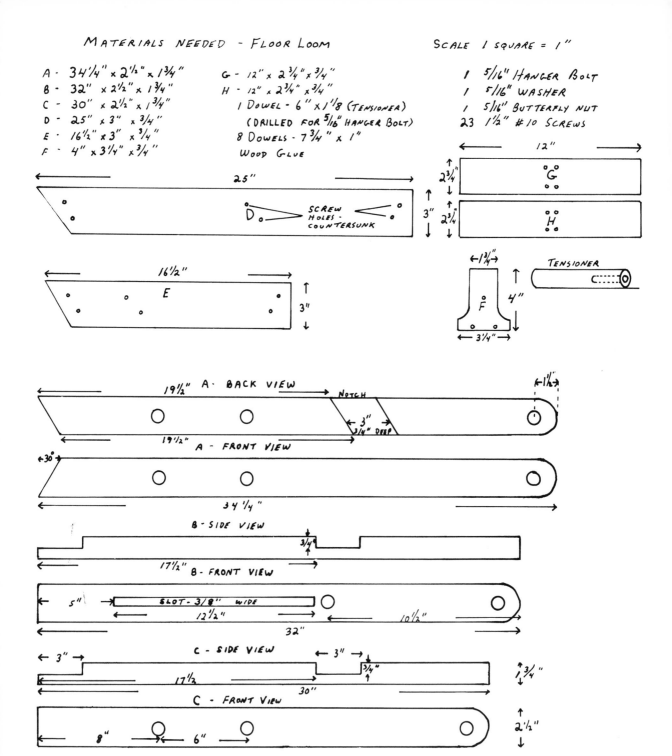

MATERIALS NEEDED - FLOOR LOOM   SCALE 1 SQUARE = 1"

A - 34¼" x 2½" x 1¾"   G - 12" x 2¾" x ¾"
B - 32" x 2½" x 1¾"   H - 12" x 2¾" x ¾"
C - 30" x 2½" x 1¾"   1 Dowel - 6" x 1⅛ (TENSIONER)
D - 25" x 3" x ¾"   (DRILLED FOR 5/16" HANGER BOLT)
E - 16½" x 3" x ¾"   8 Dowels - 7¾" x 1"
F - 4" x 3¼" x ¾"   Wood Glue

1 5/16" HANGER BOLT
1 5/16" WASHER
1 5/16" BUTTERFLY NUT
23 1½" #10 SCREWS

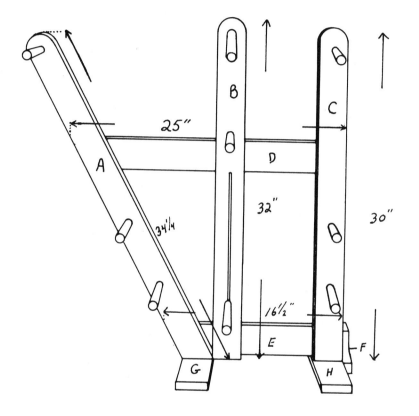

(9). LEFT, AND OPPOSITE PAGE:
Loom plans—FLOOR LOOM.

Gather These ACCESSORIES

A shuttle and a beater are the only accessories that are absolutely necessary for inkle weaving. I find it convenient, however, to have two shuttles with beater edges and a pick-up stick. The shuttle that works best for me is the middle one in illustration 10. It holds a good quantity of yarn and slips between the threads without getting caught in them. The lower edge of the shuttle is tapered so that it can be used as a beater, too.

If you cannot buy or make these accessories, many things will serve as substitutes. A table knife can be used as a beater, a pencil or small, preferably pointed, dowel as a pick-up stick, and a heavy piece of cardboard, notched on each side, can serve as a shuttle.

(*10*). Shuttles. These handsome shuttles hold a good supply of yarn, have one tapered edge which acts as a beater, and are comfortable to hold. (*Top shuttle—hand-carved gift of Steven Bress.*)

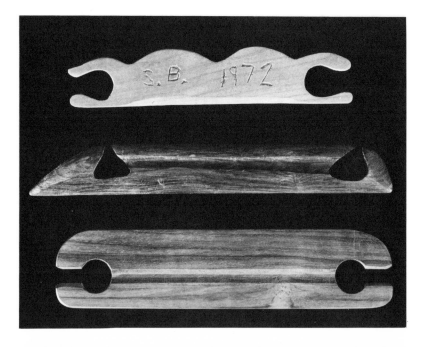

(*11*). Pick-up sticks.

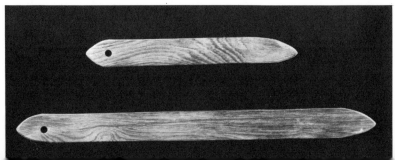

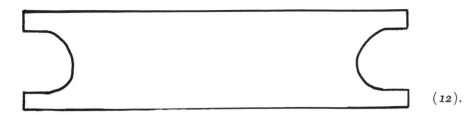

(12).

No, you don't *need* a yarn stand—but if you use spools or cones of yarn often, it does come in handy. A stand that accommodates three spools or cones is most useful. Plans for this are below, and a simpler (one-spool) stand is shown at right.

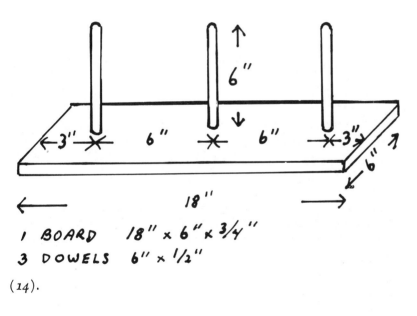

(14).

I BOARD 18" x 6" x ¾"
3 DOWELS 6" x ½"

(13).

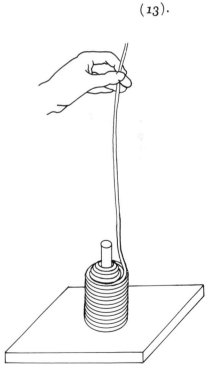

A pair of scissors and a blunt tapestry needle or bodkin are important, too. No plans for these! You can find them in the dime store.

Put on the HEDDLES

You have just bought or finished your loom and you're all excited and happy and ready to weave! But wait—where are the heddles? Alas and alack, there are none! You can't weave without them. What to do? Well, they're not hard to make— and cheer up—heddle making is a one-time thing!

MATERIALS NEEDED

For the heddles, you'll need some strong, smooth, non-elastic cord. As a veteran weaver, I would instinctively reach for the 10/5 linen on my shelf or for some waxed linen. Lacking these, I would look for some carpet warp—which is much like heavy bakery string. 3/2 pearl cotton would be my next choice. Lacking all these, I would go to the dime store and buy some heavy-weight crochet cotton. A few of these yarns are pictured on the thread chart on page 46. These are just suggestions—any smooth, strong cord that doesn't have much stretch in it, will do.

You'll also need:

    a ruler or tape measure
    a small amount of heavy cardboard or its equivalent
    a pair of scissors

Length of heddles

When they are in place on the loom, the top of the heddles should reach a little more than halfway between the heddle bar, bar H, and the top bar, bar B.

(15).

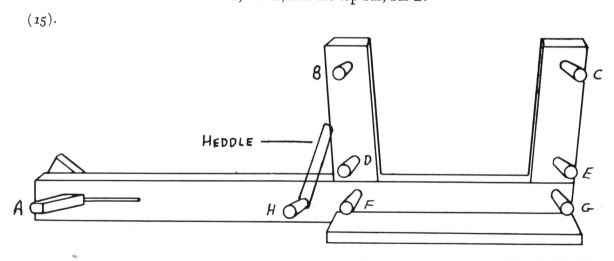

As long as a heddle is the right length, and made of strong cord, it will work and last a long time.

Methods of Making Heddles

METHOD A—is the simplest.

While weaving, these heddles work well, but may tend to slip off the end more easily than other types. They are not anchored in any way, and during the warping process, they may prove slightly elusive. When the loom is empty, you'll probably want to remove them or tie them onto the loom.

1. With your heddle cord, measure the distance between the outside of dowels H and B.
2. Add 1½ inches to this and cut the cord.
3. Fold the cord in half.
4. Cut your cardboard the length of the folded cord. *DISCARD THE CORD.*
5. Take your spool of heddle cord, and wrap a length of it around your cardboard gauge one time.
6. Remove the cord from the gauge.
7. Add 3 to 4 inches to the length of this cord and cut the cord.
8. Cut 40 more cords, the same length as the cord you've just cut.
9. Take one cord and wrap it around your cardboard gauge.
10. With the two ends, tie a square knot close to the gauge—and you've made one heddle!
11. Remove the heddle from the cardboard.
12. Repeat steps 9, 10, and 11 until all your cut cords have been converted to heddles.
13. Slip the heddles onto the heddle bar of your loom.

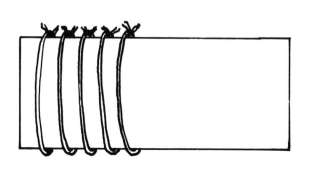

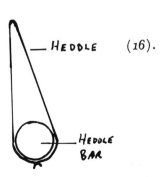

HEDDLE   (16).

HEDDLE BAR

The heddles stay on the heddle bar more securely with this method. The measurements are different and one more step is added at the end. I think it's worth the slightly extra effort.

1. Wrap your heddle cord four times around the heddle bar, bar H.
2. Bring the cord up to the top bar, bar B, cut the cord. Remove it from the loom.
3. Fold this cord in half.
4. Cut a cardboard gauge the same height as your folded string.
5. *Discard the string.*
6. Take your spool of heddle cord and wrap it around your gauge once.
7. Remove the cord from the gauge.
8. Add 3 to 4 inches to the length of this cord and cut the cord.
9. Cut 40 more cords the same length as the cord you've just cut.
10. Take one cord and wrap it around your cardboard gauge.
11. Tie the two ends in a square knot close to the gauge —and one heddle is complete.
12. Remove the heddle from the cardboard.
   Repeat steps 10, 11, and 12 until all your cut cords have been converted to heddles.

(17).

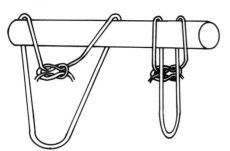

To Put Heddles on the Loom

Take one of your finished heddles and place it across the heddle bar. Have the knot face you and the loop face towards the rear of the loom.

Bring the loop around the bar, and then through the knotted end of the heddle.

Pull on the loop until the heddle is on the heddle bar snugly.

Repeat these steps until all the heddles are on.

In method C, the heddles are attached onto the loom most securely. A continuous yarn is used for this.

1. Measure the distance between the heddle bar, bar H and the top bar, bar B.
2. Divide this distance in half and add one inch. This will be the height of your cardboard gauge.
3. Cut your cardboard gauge the height derived at in #2, and make it as wide as your heddle bar.
4. Tie your heddle cord around the heddle rod securely.
5. Put your cardboard gauge against the heddle bar.
6. Bring the cord around the cardboard and back to the rod.
7. Hitch the cord around the bar three times (see diagram below).

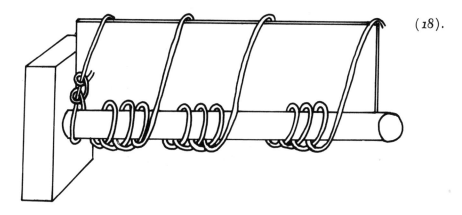 (18).

Repeat steps 6 and 7 until you have made 50 heddles.

8. Leave several inches and cut the cord.
9. Tie the end of the cord securely around the heddle bar.
10. Gently bend the cardboard gauge and slip the heddles off it.

II. *Warp Your Loom*

Now you're ready to choose a pattern and some pretty yarn and start warping your loom. I'll give general directions for warping now. Directions for changing colors and designing patterns will follow this.

Before beginning, check to see if the skein, tube, or cone that you're working with will fit through the heddles. If it doesn't, wind some off into a ball that will fit through. A yarn stand (see page 13) or a deep dish, bowl or pot for each different color is helpful in keeping your threads from tangling.

On an inkle loom, the warp must be able to be moved forward and around freely. In effect, you are making a convoluted circle. The circuit that is formed must *always* be open. Therefore, no yarn is ever wrapped completely around any dowel.

To Warp the table loom pictured:

(19a).

    1. Loosen the tension bar, and extend it out as far as it will go (see diagram below).

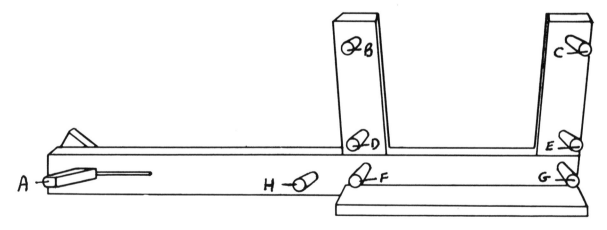

2. Wrap your first thread around a thumbtack at the front of the loom.
3. Now, bring the thread over the front bar, bar A, through the first string heddle, over the top bar, bar B, around the back bar, bar C, around bar D, then bar E, bar F, bar G, and back to the front bar. (*19b*).

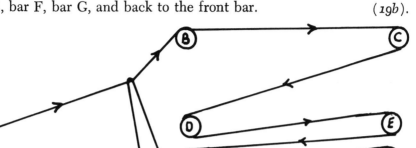

4. The second thread goes over the front bar, bar A, under the top bar, bar B, and then continues around the exact same path as the first thread. (*19c*).

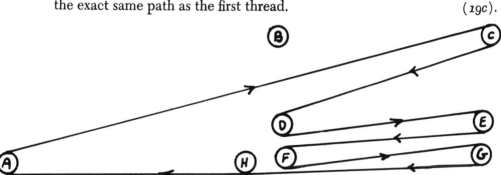

Steps 3 and 4 are repeated until there is a color change.

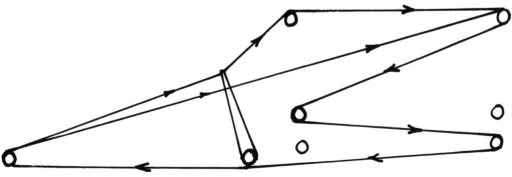

(*19d*). Pathway for a shorter warp.

To Warp the Floor Loom pictured:

(20a).

1. Put the tension bar in a position to make the threads most taut. (DIAGRAM) (This position will vary with different looms.)

A

B

C

HEDDLE BAR

E

D

TENSIONER

G

F

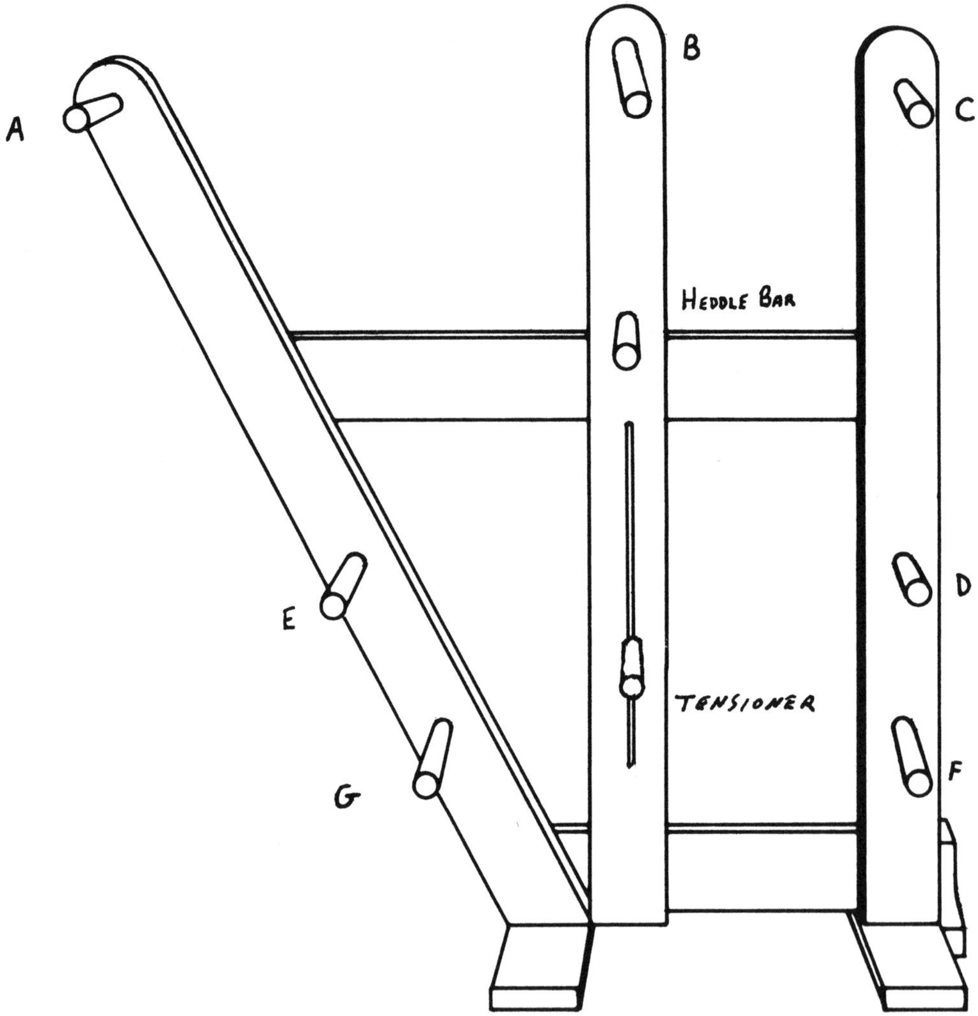

2. Wrap your first thread around a thumbtack at the front of the loom.
3. Bring the thread over the front bar, bar A, through the first string heddle, over the top bar, bar B, around the back bar, bar C, down to the bar right below this,

bar D, over to bar E, then bar F, over the tensioner, around bar G, and back to the front bar (see above).

(20b).

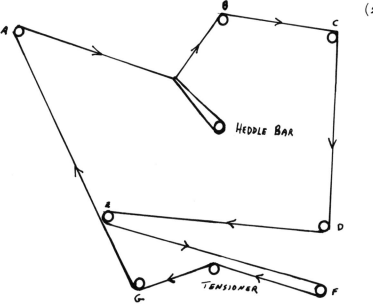

4. The next thread goes over the front bar, bar A, under the top bar, bar B, around the back bar, bar C, and then continues along the same path as the first thread.

(20c).

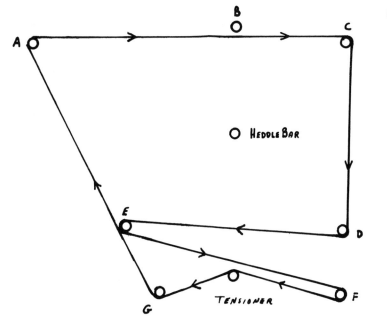

Steps 3 and 4 are repeated until there is a color change.

(*20d*). Pathway for a shorter warp.

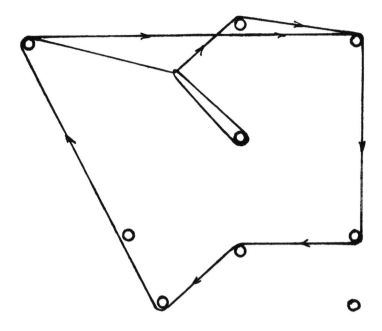

To Change Colors

METHOD A

1. Cut the first color off at the front bar, leaving a few extra inches for tying.
2. Tie the second color onto the first color on the outside of the front bar. (I use a square knot here, but any knot that will not come out under tension will work.)

Repeat these steps whenever a color change occurs.

(*21*).

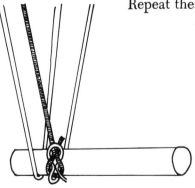

To end, remove the first thread from the thumbtack. Tie the first thread to the last thread, maintaining the same tension as the rest of the warp.

When the first few rows of weaving are completed, the crossed threads will straighten out.

METHOD B

Many people feel this is a quicker method of changing colors. A few thumbtacks at the front of the loom are needed for this method.

1. Wrap the first color around the first thumbtack a few times. WRAP—DO NOT TIE. This will keep the thread in place and under tension.
2. Wrap the second color around the second thumbtack.
3. Continue warping as before.
4. When this color is not needed, wrap it around the second thumbtack a few times.

    Repeat these steps for each new color that is added.
5. When a color that has been used previously is used again, *UNWRAP IT* from its thumbtack, and continue to warp in the usual manner. *DO NOT FORGET TO UNWRAP* THE CORD FROM ITS THUMBTACK.

(22).

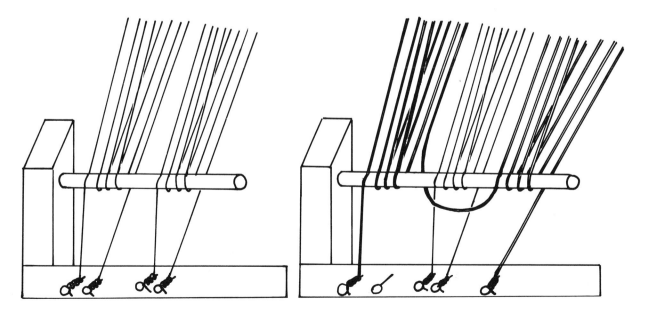

To end:

1. Cut the last thread, leaving a few extra inches.
2. Remove the thread from the last thumbtack.
3. Tie these two threads together.
4. Unwrap the next two threads and tie them together.

Continue this way until all the ends are tied off. When the first few rows of weaving are completed, the crossed threads will straighten out.

A Note on Knots

A knot within your warp will spoil the appearance of your finished piece and weaken the fabric. If you notice a knot in your thread as you are warping:

Cut that thread above the knot and bring it back to the front bar.

Cut it again, near the front bar, leaving a few extra inches of yarn.

Tie the cut yarn and the new yarn together on the outside of the front bar.

Wind Your Shuttle—And Now, LET'S WEAVE

The weft yarn shows a bit at the edge of the inkle band. Generally, both edges of the band are the same color, and the shuttle is wound with weft yarn that matches this. That makes the weft yarn very inconspicuous. One, two, three or more strands are wound onto the shuttle at one time, depending upon the effect desired. The fewer the strands, the smaller the distance between each row.

To Wind the Shuttle

1. Tie a knot around one prong of the shuttle.
2. Wind the weft around and around between points A & B.

24

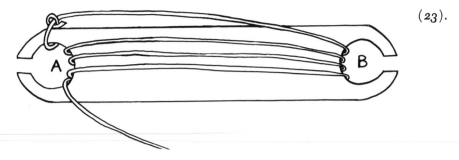

3. Continue winding until the shuttle is comfortably full. Since you want to be able to pass it between the opening, or shed, easily—don't have it bulge too much.

To Weave

Your loom is warped.
Your shuttle is wound.
Your heart is pounding a little harder—and you're ready to weave.

Wait a minute. Put the shuttle aside and just play with the loom first.

Reach behind the heddles with your right hand (illustration 24a). Put your hand under the warp threads and push the threads up. Notice that you've made the threads separate in front of the heddles. The opening that you've formed is called a "shed."

(24a).

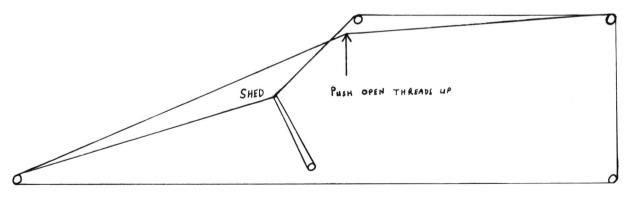

SHED PUSH OPEN THREADS UP

Now reach behind the heddles with your left hand (illustration 24b). Put your hand on top of the warp threads and push the threads down. A second opening, or shed, has been formed.

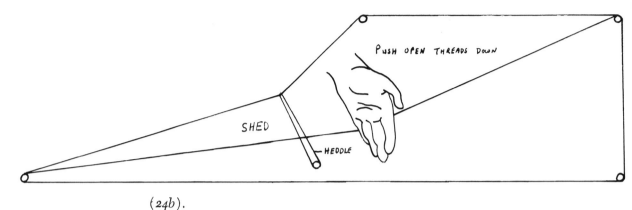

PUSH OPEN THREADS DOWN

SHED

— HEDDLE

(24b).

(25).

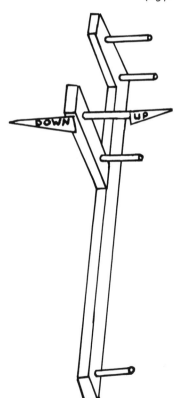

DOWN

UP

The threads in the heddles remain stationary during the weaving process, and the threads between them, in the open areas, do all the moving.

When you're weaving, these two steps are repeated over and over again, and the shuttle is passed through each shed. Pretty soon, a piece of cloth begins to form.

Now, the weaving process, step by step:

First, you might like to post two "flags" for yourself. On two small pieces of paper, or masking tape, write the words—"UP" and "DOWN." Tape "DOWN" on the post on the left side of the loom; tape "UP" on the tip of the top dowel on the right side.

To Weave (to begin the band):
1. Reach behind the heddles with your right hand.
2. Put your hand under the warp threads, and push the threads up.
3. Pass the shuttle through the shed from left to right. Leave a few-inch tail of yarn hanging out on the left side.
4. Reach behind the heddles with your left hand.

26

5. Put your hand on top of the warp threads and push the threads down.
6. Put the shuttle into the shed from right to left.
7. Beat the previous row down firmly.
8. Pass the shuttle completely through the shed.
9. Take the yarn that is hanging out from the previous row, and put it through the shed that is still open.
10. Draw the warp threads together by gently pulling on the two weft threads. *Don't* squeeze the threads tightly together. *Do* see to it that the warp threads are touching one another and that the weft doesn't show between them.

To Weave—Plain Weave:
11. Reach behind the heddles with your right hand.
12. Put your hand under the warp threads, and push the threads up.
13. Put the shuttle into the shed, from left to right.
14. Beat the previous row down firmly.
15. Pass the shuttle completely through.
16. Reach behind the heddles with your left hand.
17. Put your hand on top of the warp threads and push the threads down.
18. Put the shuttle into the shed from right to left.
19. Beat the previous row down firmly.
20. Pass the shuttle completely through.

Repeat steps 11–20 over and over again.

Pretty soon these motions become almost completely automatic. Your "UP" and "DOWN" flags can then be discarded.

I have said that you should beat the previous row of weaving down "firmly." To some, "firmly" means to beat with all one's muscle power—and more; to others, it's a love tap. Try to find some ground between these two extremes. Most of all, be consistent.

Briefly, the motions are:
1. Push the threads up.
2. Beat.
3. Pass the shuttle through.
4. Push the threads down.
5. Beat.
6. Pass the shuttle through.

Selvedges

I suspect you're fretting because your edges or selvedges are uneven. If they're even, and you're a beginner, you're rare indeed.

For better selvedges: As you draw the weft through the shed with one hand, guide it with the thumb and index finger of your other hand. Do not release the thread from your fingers until it is snugly in place at the selvedge. It will take a little practice before you're really satisfied with the selvedges.

Bringing More Warp Forward

Very soon, your weaving will get close to the heddles and the shed opening will become too small for comfort. It's time to bring more warp forward.
1. Release the tension bar a little.
2. Place one hand on the warp threads in front of the heddles, and one hand on the warp threads below the front bar.
3. Gently pull the warp forward a little.
4. Stop. Gently push the heddles back into place.
5. Gently pull the warp forward again.
6. Stop when the woven portion is about two inches in front of the front bar.
7. Retension the warp—and continue weaving.

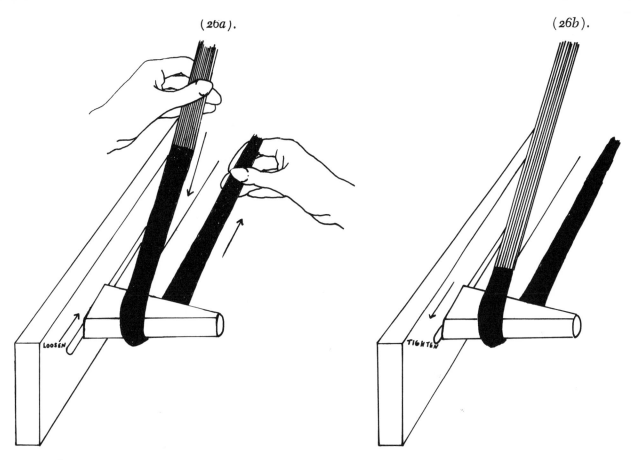

(26a).   (26b).

Take-up

The more you weave, the shorter your warp threads become. From time to time, you will need to release the tension bar a bit.

Why does this "take-up" of the warp occur and shorten the warp yarns? Well, at first the warp threads are just flat. When you put a weft thread between the warp yarns, the warp yarns envelop or curve around the weft.

(27).

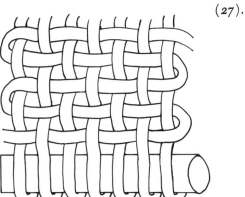

This curve takes up more yarn than the flat yarn did. The more weft shots, the more curves, and the shorter the warp becomes. This is most noticeable in less elastic yarns, such as linen. Some wools are so elastic that you never notice any take-up.

Splicing Weft Threads

Eventually, your shuttle will run out of yarn. Rewind it. Put it through the *same shed* as the previous thread. Change sheds and beat extra hard. Clip the ends short. The splice will hardly be noticeable.

(28).

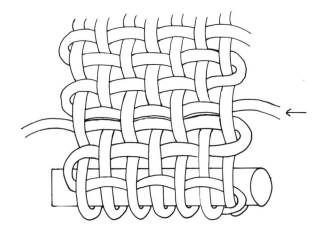

If, however, you are using several strands of yarn for weft, it would be best to cut out one or two strands from the end of the old yarn and the beginning of the new yarn. The splice would then be less bulky and look more like the previous rows.

Removing the Band from the Loom

Before you know it, there are just a few inches of warp left unwoven. At this point, it becomes difficult to make a good shed or opening. Struggle on for another inch or so, if you please—or stop before a struggle ensues. Perhaps you'll be able to use the unwoven warp threads decoratively later on.

Now, cut the weft thread from the shuttle, leaving a tail of about 12 inches, and

either (1.)

> Thread the tail onto a tapestry needle.
> "Weave" the tail into the previous row or two of weaving.

(29).

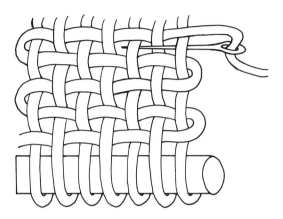

Cut the tail close to the fabric. This keeps your band from unravelling.

Now, release the tension from your loom.

Look behind the top bar and find the place where the warp threads are tied together.

Cut all the warp threads at this point.

Remove the band from the loom.

Trim the ends evenly and use it "as is," or finish it off in one of the ways suggested in Chapter X.

Or (2.)

> Release the tension from your loom.
>
> Look behind the top bar, and find the place where the warp threads are knotted together.
>
> Cut all the warp threads at this point.
>
> Remove the band from the loom.
>
> Take the last few warp threads and the tail of the weft, and make a loose overhand knot.
>
> Take the first few warp threads and make a loose overhand knot.
>
> Take a few of the center warp threads and make a loose overhand knot of them also.

This keeps the ends from ravelling. If this is to be a permanent finish for your band, tighten these knots. If the finish is to be more elaborate, you can undo them easily when you're ready to work on it some more.

There are many interesting ways to finish off your bands. See Chapter VII for some ideas.

(30).

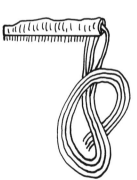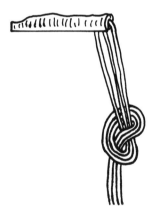

III. *PATTERNS*
in Plain Weave

With just three colors and 50 threads, almost a trillion, trillion different patterns can be formed for inkle bands! All this can be done in just the simplest type of weave there is—plain weave.

Plain weave is produced by the weaving method described on page 27.

That is: Push the open threads down.
>Beat.
>Pass the shuttle through with the weft thread.

>Push the open threads up.
>Beat.
>Pass the shuttle through with the weft thread.

These two basic operations are repeated over and over again.

If you look carefully at a plain woven inkle band, you will notice that the only threads that show are the warp threads. Yes, you do see a bit of the weft on the edges, but this is negligible. A fabric of this type is called a warp-faced fabric. The pattern is formed by the periodic changing of colors in the warp. The bands can be bright and bold or subtle and subdued.

Does it seem possible that so many different patterns can be formed on such a simple set-up? It's hard to run out of new ideas! That's the fun of designing for inkle weaving.

Drafting or Pattern Notation

The simplest and the plainest pattern would be a solid color band. To warp this, you would use just one color throughout. You would put the first thread through a heddle, the second thread between the heddles or in the "open" spaces, and repeat these two steps until the band was the desired width. Rather than write this out in words, this can be written in a simple, notation form. Let's assume the band is to be yellow and 21 threads wide.

Here's a grid with 2 rows, and a total of 21 spaces. The bottom row represents the threads that go through the heddles on the loom. The top row represents the threads that go between the heddles—or in the open spaces. Since all the threads, heddle and open, are yellow, the grid—or draft to represent this, will look like this:

(31).

O	Y Y Y Y Y Y Y Y Y Y
H	Y Y Y Y Y Y Y Y Y Y Y

You read this draft up and down, from left to right:

(32).

O	2 4 6 8 10 12 14 16 18 20
H	1 3 5 7 9 11 13 15 17 19 21

Surely, if you can count to 21, you hardly need to have a draft for such a simple band. Bands can be considerably more complex, though, and it is a big help to be able to read and design patterns using this system.

Let's go on to vertical stripes. Vertical stripes are merely a variation of a solid color band. Instead of a completely solid color, you have a solid colored area followed by other solid colored areas.

(33).

O	R R R W W W W W B B W W R R R
H	R R R W W W W W B B W W R R R R

The draft tells you to thread the loom like this:
Thread 1—Red—through the heddle
    "   2—Red—   "   " open space
    "   3—Red—   "   " heddle

"   4—Red—   "   " open space
"   5—Red—   "   " heddle
"   6—Red—   "   " open space

Now put the red thread aside (instructions for this on page 22) and start the white thread.

Thread 7—White—heddle
"   8—White—open

and so on until thread 17—

Thread 17—Blue—heddle
"   18—Blue—open
"   19—Blue—heddle
"   20—Blue—open

Put the blue aside, and pick up the white again.

Thread 21—White—heddle
"   22—White—open

and etc.

Horizontal Stripes look like this:

(*34*).

O	W	W	W	W	W	W	W	W	W	W	W	W	W	W
H	B	B	B	B	B	B	B	B	B	B	B	B	B	B

To warp:

Thread 1—Black—through the heddle
"   2—White—open space
"   3—Black—heddle
"   4—White—open

Continue in this manner for the width of the band.

Patterns and drafts are composed of vertical, horizontal, and interrupted stripes. They are more or less complex—but they are all read and interpreted in the same way.

You may have noticed that in this method of draft notation, the draft shows rather visually what the pattern on the loom will actually look like. In reality, however, the threads of the finished band are not exactly one above the other, but are rather more like this:

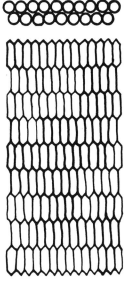

(*35a*). End view.

(*35b*). Surface of woven fabric.

Therefore, a narrow, "straight" line will come out a bit wavy. The wider the area of one color, the less noticeable the distortion.

Another point to remember is this. The weft does show a bit at either selvedge edge. If the selvedges on both sides are the same color, the weft thread can be this color, too, and will hardly be seen at all.

The basic patterns look like this:

(36). Note: The drafts for the design elements merely show how a pattern is composed. You may need to adjust the number of threads in each section to suit your warp yarns.

(*36/1*). Solid color. (A = any color)

O	A A A A A
H	A A A A A etc. for the entire width of your band.

(*36/2a*).　　　(*36/2b*).　　　(*36/2c*).　　　(*36/2d*).　　　(*36/2e*).

(*36/2f*).　　　　　　　　(*36/2g*).

(*36/2*). Stripes. Sample draft for (*36/2a*).
(A = 1st color; B = 2nd color)

O	A A A A A A B B A A B B A A
H	A A A A A A B B A A B B A A A

(*36/3*). Stripes separated by dashes.
(A = 1st color; B = 2nd color)

```
O A A A A B B B B B B B B
H A A A A B B A B B B A B B etc.
```

(*36/4*). Stripes separated by a thin line.
(A = 1st color; B = 2nd color)

```
O A A A B A A B A A
H A A A B A A B A A etc.
```

(*36/5*). Horizontal stripes.
(A = 1st color; B = 2nd color)

```
O B B B B B B
H A A A A A A etc.
```

(*36/6*). Bars. (A = 1st color; B = 2nd color)

O	A A A B B B B B B B B B A A A
H	A A A B B A A A A A A B B A A A

(*36/7a*).   (*36/7b*).   (*36/7c*).

(*36/7*). Ladder effect—combining horizontal and vertical stripes. Sample draft for (*36/7a*). (A = 1st color; B = 2nd color)

O	A A B B B B B B B A A
H	A A A A A B B A A A A A

         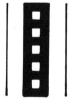

(*36/8a*).   (*36/8b*).   (*36/8c*).   (*36/8d*).

(*36/8*). Stripes with small squares. (A = 1st color; B = 2nd color)

O	A A A A B B B B B B B A
H	A A A A B B A A A B B A etc.

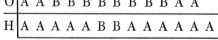

"square"

($36/9$). Checks. (A = 1st color; B = 2nd color)

O	A A A B B B B A A A B
H	B B B B A A A B B B B etc.

This is just a guide to some of the basic design elements that are possible on a plain weave inkle band. These fragments may be widened or narrowed, be repeated symmetrically or asymmetrically, be used either alone or combined. They may be woven in two, three, four or more colors. The colors may be closely related or brightly contrasted.

Designing with these elements can be fun. Graph paper and colored felt tip pens are a great help. Later on, you may prefer to design directly on the loom, but you will retain the facility of putting down, in "shorthand," patterns as they occur to you.

Here are some patterns combining the design elements.

(37). Information about these bands are in the Appendix.

($37a$).   ($37b$).   ($37c$).   ($37d$).

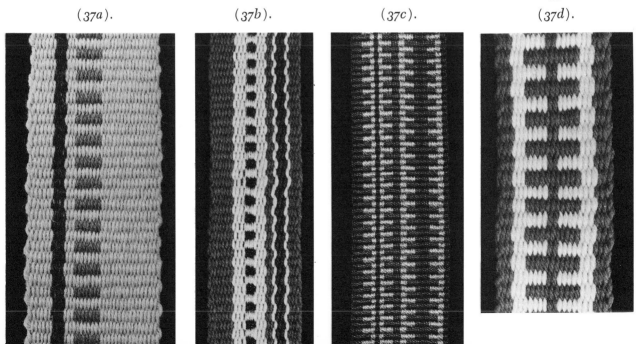

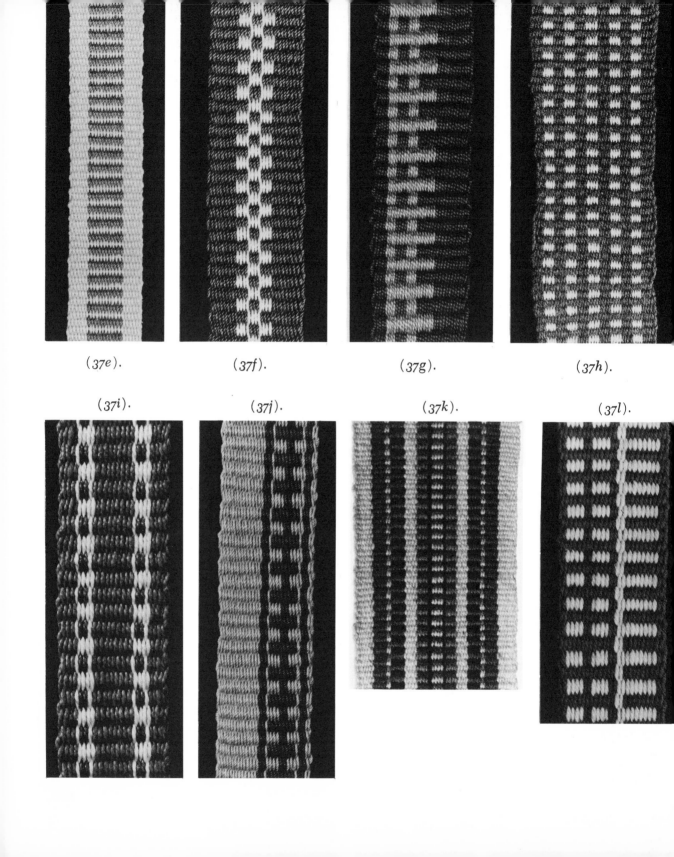

($37e$).　　　　($37f$).　　　　($37g$).　　　　($37h$).

($37i$).　　　　($37j$).　　　　($37k$).　　　　($37l$).

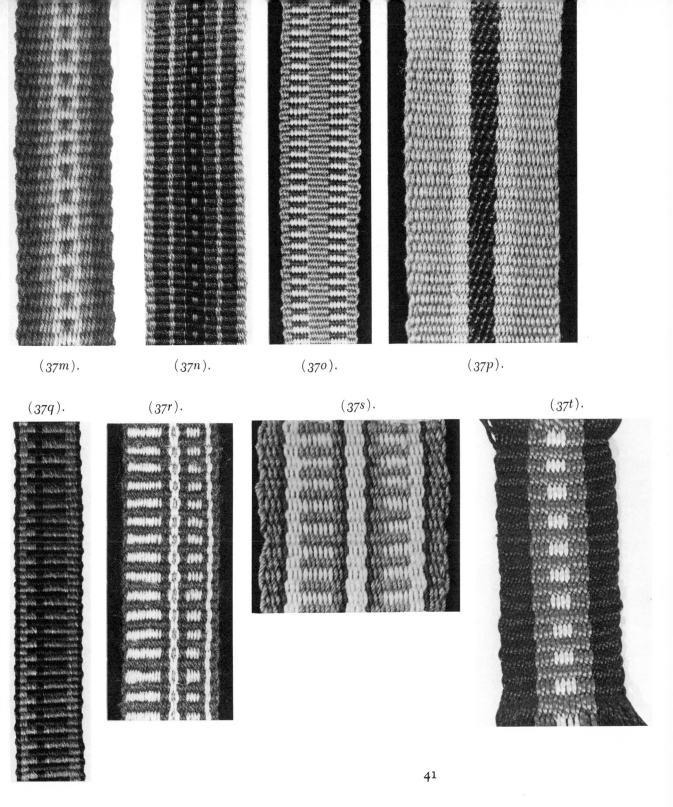

(37m).   (37n).   (37o).   (37p).

(37q).   (37r).   (37s).   (37t).

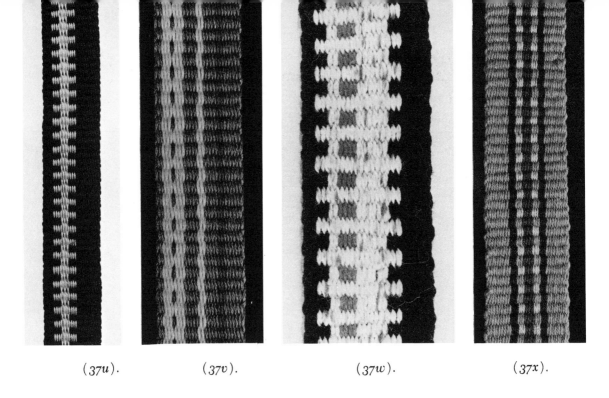

(37*u*).   (37*v*).   (37*w*).   (37*x*).

How good a designer would a computer be? Would it come up with unique designs? Would it turn out pleasing designs? Dan Bress decided to find out and presented me with a print-out of 600 patterns.

The computer has no aesthetic sense of its own. Since it must try out every idea that pops into its "head," there will be a high percentage of rejects. It's quite a thrill to stumble across one that works well—and that you may not have thought of yourself.

If computer programming appeals to you, you can have much fun feeding different programs to your favorite computer. However, it is most probable that you can explore your own mind and come up with more patterns than you will ever find time to weave!

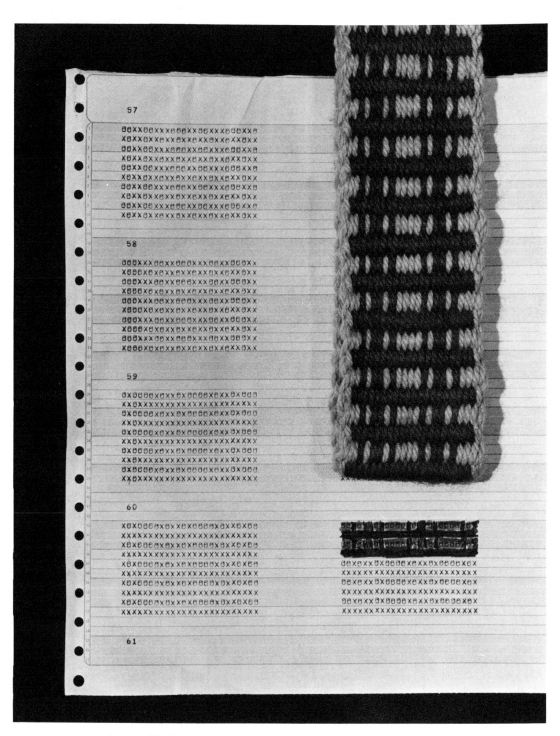

(38). Computer designed belt.
(*Programmer and weaver:*
Dan Bress.)

IV. *Choose Some YARNS*

Yarns—a weaver's palette! And there are so many kinds and colors to choose from.

A smooth, plied yarn is easiest to work with. You know what smooth is—but what is a ply? Yarn is spun from relatively short fibers into a single strand of yarn. This is called a single ply or a "singles" yarn. If you untwist it, you will see the fibers from which it was spun. Most of the familiar yarns go through another process. Two, three, four or more of the singles are twisted or plied together to make a two, three, four or more plied yarn. The commonest knitting yarns are four ply yarns. Untwist a piece and you'll see four separate strands of yarn. A singles yarn is usually not as strong as a plied yarn and cannot take as much abrasion as a plied yarn.

As you have seen, inkle bands are warp-face fabrics. The warp threads are dense and are under considerable tension. Yet, they must slip by one another often and with relative ease. This is why a smooth, plied yarn is recommended.

Textured yarns can be used, but with discretion. If you don't use too many of them, place them on the open shed only, completely surround them with smooth yarns, and baby them along a bit, you'll probably meet with success. Illustrations 40 and 41 are examples of bands using textured yarns. I think it's worth the extra effort to use them.

(39).

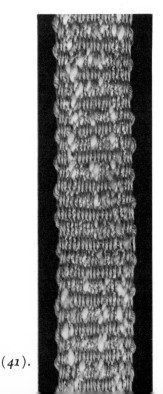

(41).

(40).

(40, 41). Bands using textured yarns.

I thoroughly recommend that you stay away from very hairy yarns and single ply yarns. I used some beautiful, heavy singles Icelandic wool in this belt (illustration 42).

(*42*). Beautiful heavy single ply wool. But—it doesn't work well for inkle weaving!

I made the pattern very simple so that the yarn would show off to good advantage. I was as gentle as gentle could be with the yarn, but to no avail. I couldn't weave it well and the yarn frayed and broke often. The photograph is of the best few inches. Please don't ask to see the rest.

I used my own hand spun, single ply, vegetable dyed yarn in this belt. The colors are soft and subtle and don't show up well in the photograph (43) but the raggedy edges do! It was very difficult to weave.

(*43*). Handspun, vegetable dyed, single ply yarn. A plied yarn would have been more successful!

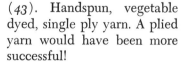

45

Yarns

Here's a sampling of some yarns and their characteristics. A multitude of other yarns are available, and many of them would work well for inkle weaving.

The chart shows individual strands of yarns full size and gives you some important information about them. In the basket are cones, tubes, and skeins of the yarns as you would find them in a shop.

(44). Yarns commonly used for inkle weaving.

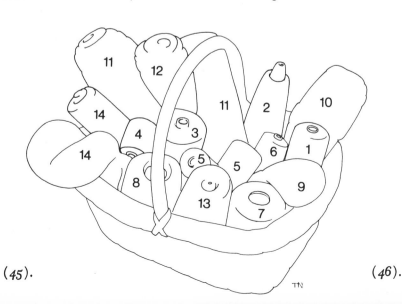

(45).

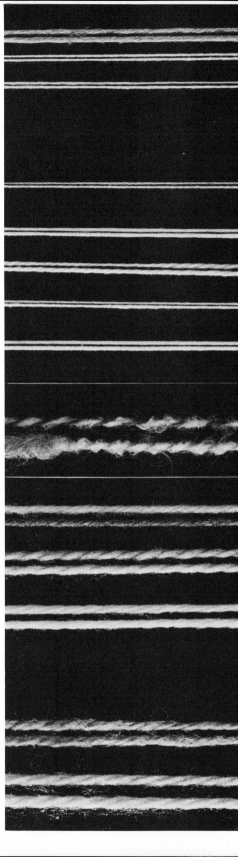

(46).

(46). OPPOSITE: Yarns commonly used for inkle weaving. Two strands of each yarn are shown. The numbers correspond to the numbers on the yarns in the basket and to the numbers on the chart that follows.

YARNS AND THEIR CHARACTERISTICS

YARN	YARDS PER	NO. OF THREADS FOR ABOUT 1″ OF FINISHED BAND	CHARACTERISTICS	WHERE AVAILABLE
1. 10/5 Linen	600 per lb.	26	Heavy, strong and non-elastic. Works easily and well. Much take-up.	Weaving Supply shops
2. 10/3 Linen	1000 per lb.	42	Medium-weight linen. Strong, non-elastic. Works well.	Weaving Supply shops
3. 10/2 Linen	1500 per lb.	48	Strong, non-elastic. Combines well with wool for pick-up techniques.	Weaving Supply shops
4. 5/2 Perle Cotton (#5)	2100 per lb. cone 262 per 2 oz. tube	52	Medium-weight cotton. Extremely wide color range available. Nice sheen. Very easy to work with.	Weaving Supply shops
5. 6 strand Floss	260 per 2 oz. tube	48	Smooth, lustrous, very easy to work with. Wide range of colors available. Gives silky appearance and feel. This is the same as embroidery floss, but it is much more economical in the 2 oz tube or pound cone.	Weaving Supply shops
6. 3/2 Perle Cotton (#3)	1260 per lb. cone 157 per 2 oz. tube	35	Heaviest weight perle cotton generally available. Very wide range of colors. Nice sheen. Very easy to work with.	Weaving Supply shops
7. Crochet Cotton, regular weight	175 per tube	57	Works easily and well. Number of colors limited.	Dime store; Knitting shops
8. Crochet Cotton, heavy weight	100 per tube	40	Works easily and well. Number of colors available are limited.	Dime store; Knitting shops
9. Textured Knitting Yarn	varies	Varies. Not recommended for whole width.	Nubs appear at frequent intervals. Will not pass through heddles easily. Use on "Open" warp. Tends to be sticky. Beautiful yarns of this type are available. Best used as an accent.	Knitting shops

YARN	YARDS PER	NO. OF THREADS FOR ABOUT 1″ OF FINISHED BAND	CHARACTERISTICS	WHERE AVAILABLE
10. 4 ply knitting worsted, synthetic, space dyed	265 per 4 oz skein	24	On the American space dyed yarns, the colors change at specific intervals. Can adjust yarns to form color patterns. (See page 85.) Is a bit more sticky than the cotton yarns, but still works well.	Dime stores, Knitting shops
11. 4 ply knitting worsted, synthetic	265 per 4 oz skein	24	Works well, but is a bit more sticky than the cottons. Many colors available.	Dime stores, Knitting shops
12. 4 ply knitting worsted, wool	approx. 255 per 4 oz. skein	22	Works well. Is a bit more sticky than the cottons. Wide range of colors available.	Dime stores, Knitting shops
13. Rug yarn, wool	Varies between brands. This one has 375 yards per pound	Varies. This one takes about 20 threads	Heavy. Works up quickly. Wide range of colors. A bit sticky, but most brands work well. Is best not to wash before weaving.	Weaving supply houses and shops
14. Rug yarn, acrylic	Varies between brands, approx. 140 per 4 oz. skein	18	Heavy. Works up quickly. Some brands are rather sticky. Good range of colors.	Dime stores, Yarn shops

Cottolin is a combination of cotton and linen, and it works well. (3200 yds. per pound) It's a bit hard to find in this country, though.

Some other yarns that might be fun to try are: jute, rayon satin cord (rattail), finer weights of knitting and weaving wools and gold lamé. And then, too, sewing threads come in a vast assortment of colors. Well, it's a thought.

V. *Explore These* TECHNIQUES

The list of interesting and innovative things that can be done on an inkle loom is long. Let's explore a few.

How About Making Some—

Picots

The edges of a band do not always have to be straight. They can be varied with picots at regular intervals

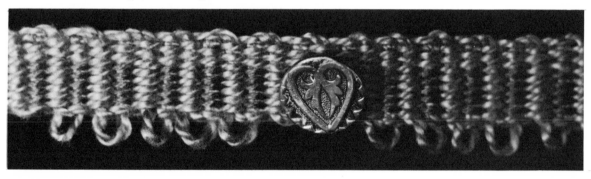

or at irregular intervals (*48*).

(*47*). ABOVE: Choker with picots at regular intervals. The antique silver button has a shank on the back (see page 81) and was woven right in.

and they might even form the heading for a wall hanging.

(*49*). Picots grace the top of this band and long strands fall below it. The free strands will be knotted into a macramé hanging, and beads will be interspersed throughout. See diagram (*58*). *Photograph— Seymour Bress.*

Picots are very simple to make, but please look over these instructions before you plunge in. *Two* shuttles and *two* weft threads are needed! One weft will act as a binder thread, and should be the same color as the edges of your band. You'll probably want a relatively fine thread for this.

The other weft will form the picots. It can be any color or weight you please.

To Weave:

    1. Pass the binder thread through a shed.

    2. *Into this same shed*, pass the picot thread, too.

50

3. Change sheds and beat firmly.
4. Pass the binder thread through and bring it close to the edge of the band as you would normally do.
5. In this same shed, pass the picot thread through. Let it extend beyond the edge of the band.

Repeat steps four and five for each picot.

If only one shuttle were used, the edge warp threads would loosen and fill in the picots. The picots would disappear and you'd be left with a sloppy looking band.

If the picots are made at the edge of each row, they would appear like this:

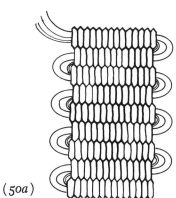

(50a)

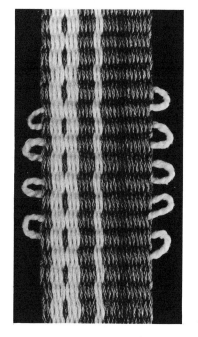

(50b).

If done on one edge only, the "picot" weft will show a little bit on the other selvedge. Your choice of color for the picots may be affected by this.

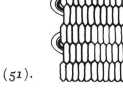

(51).

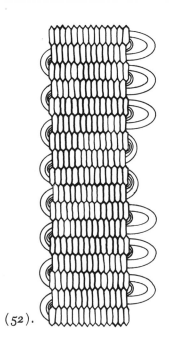

(52).

Picots can be placed regularly, irregularly, can be all the same size, or vary in size.

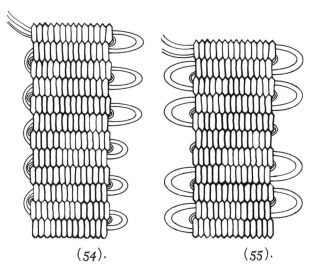

(54).   (55).

(53).

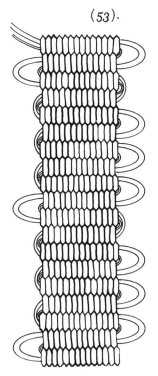

A picot doesn't have to be the height of just one row. If you want it bigger:

Weave one row with the binder weft and the "picot" weft.

Put the picot weft aside.

Weave a few rows with the binder weft ONLY.

Weave a row with the binder weft *and* the picot weft.

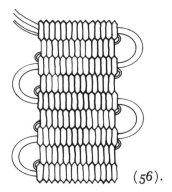

(56).

You might like to use a stiff or heavy yarn for a large picot. How about jute, rayon satin cord (rattail), waxed linen, chenille, seine twine, or even some copper, aluminum or telephone wire?

Here are some more ideas to experiment with:

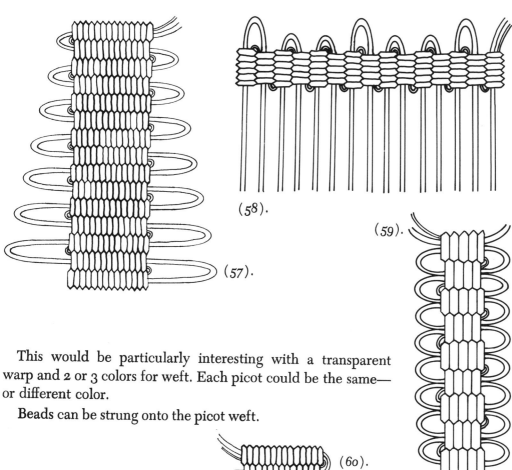

(58).

(59).

(57).

This would be particularly interesting with a transparent warp and 2 or 3 colors for weft. Each picot could be the same— or different color.

Beads can be strung onto the picot weft.

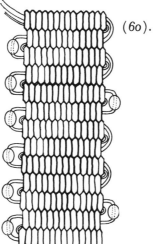

(60).

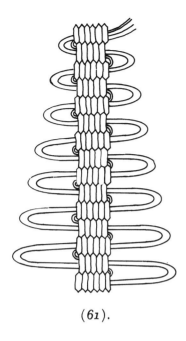

(61).

With stiff, colored telephone or bell wire, you have a trimmable tree. On a very narrow warp, these could be used for jewelry; on a wider warp, they could be used for tree decorations or door trim.

Fringes

At what point does a row of picots become an uncut fringe? When you run out of things to worry about, ponder about that for a while! In the meanwhile, let's see how to make fringes and some of the things that can be done with them.

Fringes occur rather naturally at the beginning and end of a woven piece. The kind of fringe I'm discussing here, however, is the kind that is deliberately woven into the sides of a piece. The method of weaving is much the same as for picots.

At least two different weft yarns are needed. The shuttle will usually carry a fine, binder weft which will be the same color as the edge warp threads. The binder thread will then be quite inconspicuous. The other weft or wefts will make the fringes. It doesn't matter whether or not this is carried on a shuttle. If the fringe is to be even, you'll probably want to have a gauge. The gauge should be a few inches wide and the length of your fringe. A piece of cardboard makes a good gauge.

To Weave a Fringe on One Side of An Inkle Band:

Pass the binder thread through a shed.

In this same shed, pass the fringe weft through.

Change sheds and beat firmly.

Pass the binder thread through and bring it close to the band—as you would normally do.

Put your gauge against the selvedge of your band.

(62).

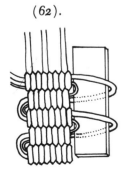

Bring the fringe weft around the gauge and into the same shed as the binder weft.

Repeat these steps as many times as desired.

Remove the gauge often. If it's flexible, bend it slightly and it will come out easily.

If the binder weft were omitted, the selvedge threads would loosen and become straggly.

The fringe I've described so far occurs on just one side of the band. The fringe weft will show a bit at the other side. This may or may not matter to you. It's just a point to remember when choosing fringe colors and weights.

(63).

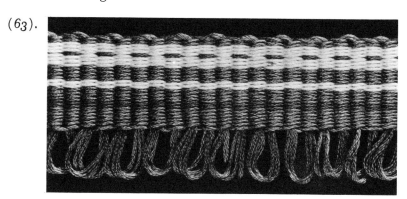

Fringes can be simple and short or long and dramatic; they can be cut or uncut, full or sparse.

(64).

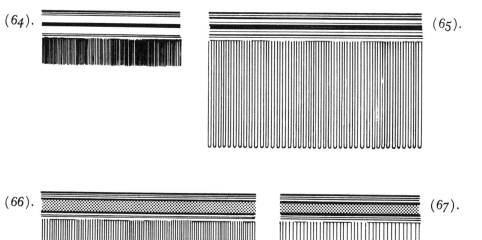

(65).

(66).

(67).

They can be on one side or both sides.

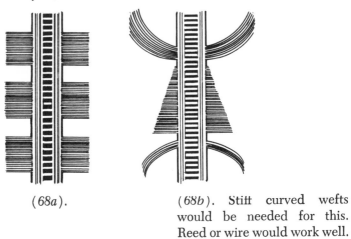

(68a).

(68b). Stiff curved wefts would be needed for this. Reed or wire would work well.

Sometimes they can be even and sometimes they can be shaped.

(69).

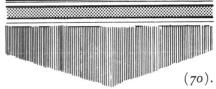

(70).

They may be solid along the whole length of the band, or grouped in areas.

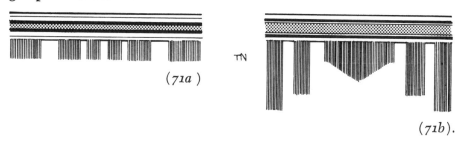

(71a)

(71b).

The colors can be the same or different throughout; the yarns may be the same as the warp or completely different.

After it is taken off the loom, a long fringe can be converted into an intricate piece of macramé. It can also be braided, twisted, and have beads added to it.

(72). Metamorphosis of an inkle band with a long fringe into a choker with a macramé center.

Adding Some Rods

Rigid Wefts

We usually think of weft materials as being soft and pliable. Usually they are—but rigid materials can be used, too.

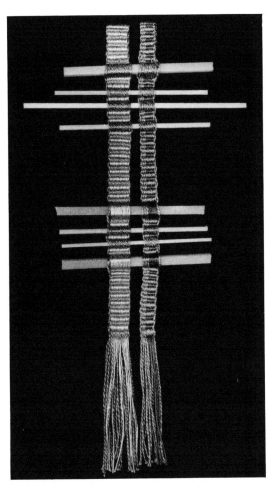

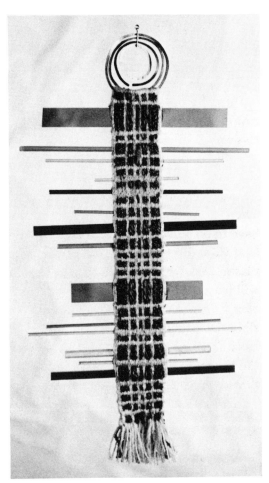

(73). Tiny hanging with plastic bars woven in. 12″ long. *Photograph—Seymour Bress.*

(74). Bright little hanging with plastic bars and rods woven in randomly. It is topped off with rings from a large dangling earring.

Colorful plastic rods, dowels, bamboo, and twigs are some examples of these. Besides the rigid weft, you'll need a binder weft. The binder weft should be a yarn that is similar in weight or smaller than the warp threads, and the same color as the selvedges.

To Weave:

> Pass the binder thread through a shed.
> Into this same shed, place your rigid weft.
> Change sheds and beat very firmly.

Repeat as desired.

I usually put at least one row of plain weave between each row of stiff materials. I think the rigid materials are more secure this way.

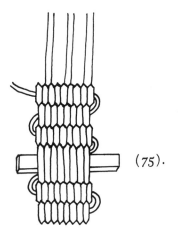

(75).

The Christmas tree in illustration 76 is still on the loom. There is no more weaving space on the loom, and the tree will have to be moved forward. You'll notice that some of the plastic bars extend beyond the side of the loom quite a bit. Since the plastic bars won't be able to pass around the front dowel, they will have to be pushed—gently—to the right. I'll push the band over a bit, too, to give the plastic bars as much space as possible. Of course, I'll move them back after I've woven a few more trees and have taken them off the loom. I'll then turn the tree over and put a dab of epoxy cement on each selvedge thread that has a plastic rod beneath it.

(76). A Christmas tree is being woven on this loom. See text (left) for further details. *Photograph—Seymour Bress.*

(77). Christmas tree. Small plastic bars and rods form the branches.

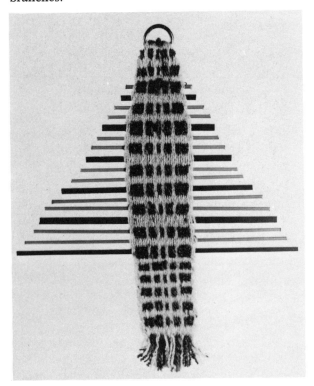

(78). This bright black, red, and gold band is flanked with red plastic bars and clusters of fine plastic rods. It is topped with the dangle part of a long aluminum earring. *Photograph —Seymour Bress.*

Shaped pieces of wood, feathers, leather, wire, copper tubes, reeds, and dried flowers are some other materials you might like to try.

60

(79). Narrow hatband with feathers woven in. *Photograph —Seymour Bress.*

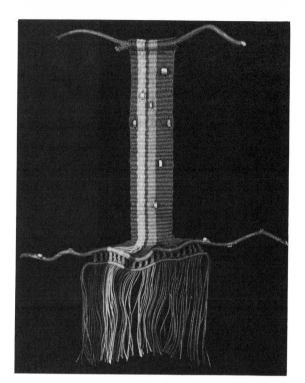

(80). Grapevine branches at top and bottom transform a straight and narrow inkle band.

Wrapping and Binding with Macramé

So far, everything we've discussed has been quite solid and closed in. Sometimes it's desirable to have some open areas. There are several ways you can do this.

(81). Bright blue and green hanging with bells, bars and wrapped warp threads.

(82). Close-up of the wrapped warp threads in the blue and green hanging.

You can achieve the open effect in illustrations 81 and 82 either by wrapping some unwoven warp ends or by square knotting around them.

First, end off your weft thread at the place where you want your open area to begin. Then, choose a yarn that you'd like to cover some warp ends with. Here's an opportunity for you to vary your color scheme. The wrapping or knotting yarn does not have to be the same color or weight of either your warp or your weft. It should be relatively smooth and strong, though. The warp threads are dense. In order to create an opening, several warp threads need to be used as the core for the wrapping or knotting.

To Wrap

Cut a piece of yarn many times longer than the length of the area to be wrapped.

Fold the yarn unevenly as in the diagram.

Place the folded yarn next to the *warp threads* to be wrapped.

Take the longer strand and bring it around the warp threads.

Keep on wrapping around and around, always placing the wrapping yarn above the previous turn.

When the wrapped portion is as long as desired, slip the end of the wrapping yarn through the loop.

Pull on the "tail" at the bottom of the wrapped section.

When the top end is securely within the wrapped section, both ends can be trimmed.

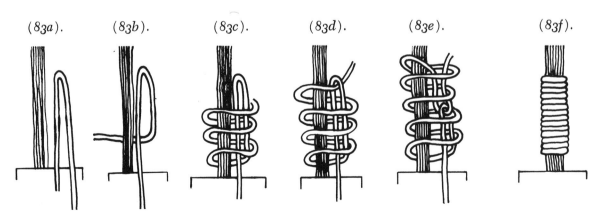

(83a).   (83b).   (83c).   (83d).   (83e).   (83f).

Square Knotting or Macramé

If you're familiar with macramé, you'll see that a similar effect can be achieved by square knotting around several of the warp threads.

In this case you would:

    Cut a piece of yarn about eight times the length of the warp threads you are going to cover.

    Fold it in half.

    Place the center fold under a group of warp threads as on the diagram. (A)

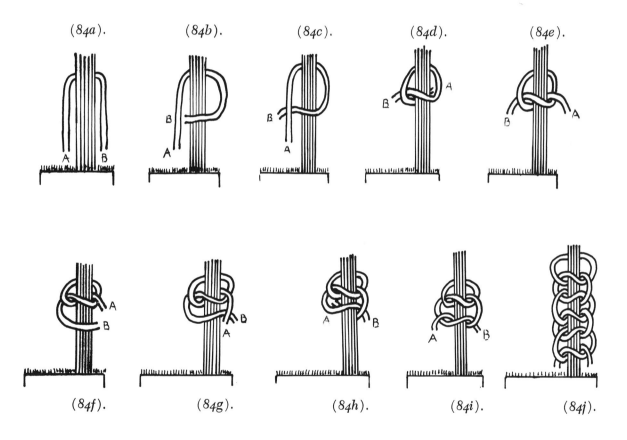

(84a).   (84b).   (84c).   (84d).   (84e).

(84f).   (84g).   (84h).   (84i).   (84j).

Use a few warp threads as core cords.

63

Take the cord on the right, cord B, and place it over and
to the left of the warp yarns you are using for the
core. (B)

Drop cord B.

Take the cord on the left, cord A, and place it on top of
cord B. (The figure you have now made resembles a
backwards "4.") (C)

Bring cord A under the warp yarns and through the loop
on the right. (D)

Pull cords A and B to tighten. (E)

This completes the first half of the square knot. The second
half is the same as the first, but in reverse.

Cord B is now on the left. Bring it over and to the right
of your core cords. (F)

Drop cord B.

Place cord A on top of cord B. (The figure you have now
made resembles the number "4.") (G)

Bring cord A under the core cords, and through the loop
on the left. (H)

Tighten by pulling cords A and B. (I)

This completes one square knot.

Make one square knot below the other until you reach the
woven part of the band. (J)

After making several square knots a rhythm will begin to
form:

First Half—

    Start with the right cord:

Right	OVER	core cords
Left	OVER	cord B
	UNDER	core cords
	& THROUGH	loop

Second Half—

Left	OVER	core cords
Right	OVER	cord A
	UNDER	
	& THROUGH	loop.

Or—

> Over, over, under, and through
> Over, over, under, and through

With a tapestry needle, weave the ends of the yarn into the woven part of the band, and clip them short.

Slits

Here's still another way to form some openings in your weaving. Slits are easy to make and they can serve either a decorative or functional purpose.

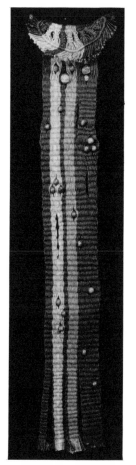

(85). Linen hanging with slits, tabs, and beads woven in.

(86). Close-up of a woven-in slit.

(87). BELOW: "Coming and Going" necklace. A long slit forms the head opening. One end hangs down in front, the other in the back. *Photograph —Seymour Bress.*

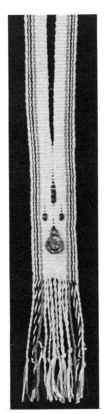

(88). LEFT: Close-up of the formal end of the necklace. *Photograph—Seymour Bress.*

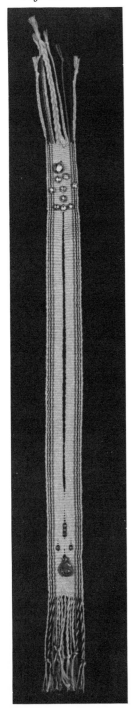

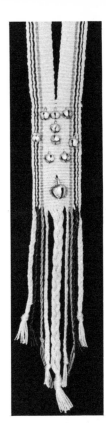

(89). RIGHT: Close-up of the noisy end of the necklace. *Photograph—Seymour Bress.*

To make a slit in your weaving:

Two shuttles wound with the same weight yarn are needed.

    Weave with one shuttle until you reach the row where your slit is to begin.

    In the next shed—

        weave all across the row with shuttle A.

        weave all across the row with shuttle B.

    Change sheds and beat hard.

    In this shed:

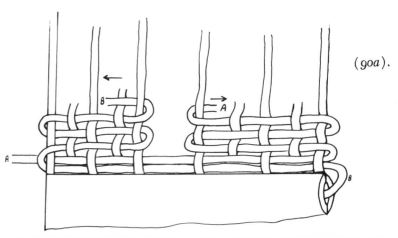

(90a).

weave all across with shuttle A.

weave part way across with shuttle B. Bring this shuttle to the surface where you want the slit to occur.

Change sheds and beat.

In this shed:

Weave with shuttle A up to the slit. Bring the shuttle to the surface.

Weave with shuttle B from the slit to the selvedge.

Change sheds and beat.

In this shed:

Weave with shuttle B up to the slit. Bring the shuttle to the surface.

Weave with shuttle A from the slit to the other selvedge.

Continue in this way until your slit is as long as you desire.

To End—or close up the other side of the slit:

In the same shed, weave both wefts to the same outside selvedge.

Change sheds and beat.

In this shed, weave all across with both wefts. Cut one off.

Continue weaving with just one shuttle.

Note: If your slit is for decorative purposes, you might want it to be rather open. If so, then deliberately pull the wefts tight at the point where the slit is forming.

Note, too, that you will need to add one more weft thread for each additional slit you make in one area.

With a slit or two at one end, and a big, unusual button at the other, you'd have a rather special belt.

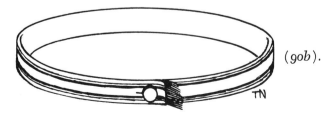

(90b).

And here's a purse made with three strips:

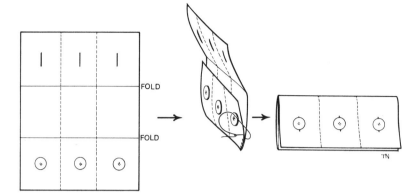

(*91*).

Tabs

Actually, a tab is an incomplete slit. Tabs can be made at the beginning and/or the end of a piece.

(*92*). Close-up of the tabs at the end of the hanging in photograph (*85*).

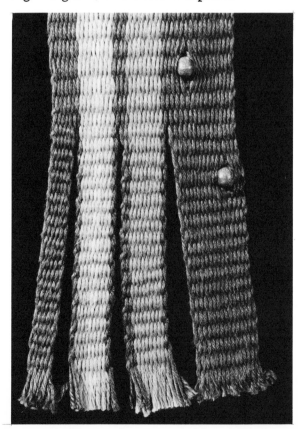

To make a tab at the end of a piece:

Follow the directions for making a slit but do not close
it up at the bottom. End the wefts separately, in the
same manner as you would end any weft thread.

To make two tabs at the beginning of a piece:

Start with two shuttles wound with yarn of equal weight.

Open the first shed.

In this shed:

Weave part way across the row with shuttle A. Bring
this shuttle to the surface where you want one tab
to end.

Enter the second shuttle, shuttle B, at the point where
you ended the first tab.

Change sheds and beat.

In this shed:

Weave with shuttle B up to the slit. Bring the shuttle
to the surface.

Weave with shuttle A from the slit to the selvedge.

Change sheds and beat.

In this shed:

Weave with shuttle A up to the slit. Bring the shuttle
to the surface.

Weave with B from the slit to the other selvedge.

Continue in this way until your tab is as long as you desire.

To Close Up the Bottom of the Tabs

In the same shed, weave both wefts to the same outside
selvedge.

Change sheds and beat.

In this shed, weave all across with both wefts. Cut one
off.

Continue weaving with just one shuttle.

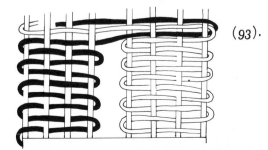

(93).

69

To make the tabs in the necklace more defined (illustration 94), I didn't weave over all the warp threads. I omitted a few warp threads between each tab, and then hid them by darning them into the fabric after the necklace was cut off the loom.

(94). Linen neckpiece with tabs, beads, and tie for the neck woven in. *Ceramic disc —Noel Clark.*

Leaving Warp Unwoven in Places

Not all the warp threads need to be woven at all times. For special effects, some areas can be left unwoven. The weaving technique for this is similar to the one for making slits. Illustrations 95 and 96 are examples of this. Let's examine how the hanging in illustration 95 was woven.

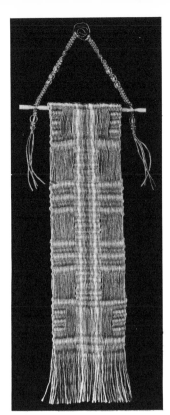

(95). To vary the pattern and color areas, some sections of this hanging have been left unwoven.

(96). Experimental hanging with some areas left unwoven.

TOP SECTION:

Two shuttles were used. One shuttle wove back and forth on the end threads on the right hand side, while another shuttle wove back and forth on the end threads on the left hand side.

The middle threads were left unwoven.

The top section was followed by a few rows of plain weave, woven from edge to edge with just one shuttle.

SECOND SECTION:

One shuttle was used. Only the middle threads were woven. The warp threads on either side were left unwoven.

The rest of the piece is just a repeat of the above, weaving over more or fewer warp yarns to vary the design.

(97). Sketch of second section of hanging, photograph (95) being woven.

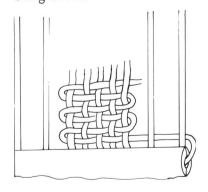

71

Of course, this technique needs to be used with discretion. Long warp floats are formed. This would be quite acceptable in a wall hanging, which doesn't get much wear—but could be impractical for a purse.

Warp floats are fun to play with. You can shift your patterns this way from one that is broken up in color, to one that has solid blocks of color. You can push beads into these areas, tie groups of threads together, and wrap or knot around some or all of the warp threads.

Tube

You can make your band into a tube as you weave! It's kind of fun to know this, and an interesting stunt to perform—but generally speaking, has little practical value.

Inkle bands are relatively narrow. When they're made into a tube, you get a skinny tube. Because of the curve, it's very hard to beat. I can't seem to think of many uses for a long, skinny, not well beaten tube!

To make a tube: You cannot beat a tube well with a flat beater. A table fork will serve as a substitute. One weft only is used and the weft is always entered from the same side. If you start weaving the tube from left to right, then the whole tube is woven from left to right. Conversely, if you start weaving from right to left, the whole tube is woven from right to left.

1. Open a shed.
2. Beat.
3. Bring the shuttle around to the same side you wove from in the previous row.
4. Pass the shuttle through this shed from this same side.
5. Open the other shed.
6. Beat firmly with a fork.

Repeat steps 3–6 over and over again until the tube is the length you desire.

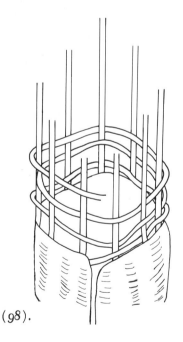

(98).

72

Illustration 99 is an example of a tube used decoratively in a hanging. After the tubular part, the hanging was woven flat again. In order to keep this part flat, a copper bar was woven in a little below the tube. The idea is sound, but is the result as interesting to look at as it sounds?

(99). Linen hanging with a woven-in tubular section.

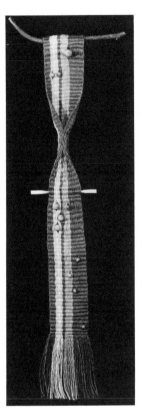

(100). Close-up of the tubular section.

Ghiordes or Rya Knot

Here's a very versatile technique. It's a knot that forms a pile on the surface of the fabric. It's called a Ghiordes Knot. Rya and Flossa pile rugs are most often made with this knot. Yes, you can make a whole rug with it—or—you can just use it in small areas. It can be used on hangings, necklaces, rugs, purses, belts, and more. It combines beautifully with other techniques.

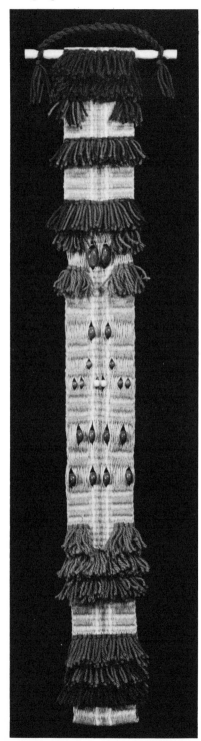

(*101*). Ghiordes knots in shades of orange, grace the surface of this long, linen hanging.

(*102*). Close-up of a group of Ghiordes knots.

Materials Needed for the Knot—relatively soft yarns that blend well with your warp. A few strands are used together to make one knot.

METHOD A:

For practice, cut three strands of yarn, each 4 inches long. (The number and length of the strands will vary according to the effect you want.)

Open a new shed.

Hold the first two warp yarns on the left with your left hand.

74

Center the strands of the Ghiordes Knot yarn over the
two warp threads you are holding.

Bring the strands on the left around and under the left
warp thread.

Bring the strands on the right around and under the right
warp thread.

All the strands of the Ghiordes Knot yarn are now between
the two warp threads.

Pull on the Ghiordes Knot you've made to tighten it and
bring it close to the woven edge of the band.

Repeat this as often as desired across the row.

Change sheds.

Beat.

Weave a few rows of plain weave before making some more
Ghiordes Knots.

(103a).　　　(103b).　　　　　(103c).

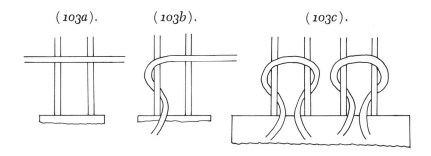

Here's another method of making the Ghiordes Knot. If the
pile knot is to be the same color(s) across the row, then this
method is faster than the other. Also, if you want a looped,
uncut pile, this is the method you'll need to use.

METHOD B:

For this method, you'll need to have a gauge the same height
as the pile you want. This can be a ruler, pick-up stick, or perhaps a piece of cardboard. It's helpful to have the gauge at
least a little wider than the width of one row. Several long
strands of yarn are used together for this method.

1. Open a shed.
2. Hold the first two warp threads in your left hand.
3. Bring the knotting yarn
    between the two warp threads
    under the left warp thread
    on top of the two warp threads
    around and under the right warp thread
    into the middle of the two warp threads.
4. Tighten this knot by pulling it towards you.
5. Place the gauge flat against the last woven row of your band.
6. Bring the knotting yarn over, around, and under the gauge.
7. Pick up the next two warp threads.

Repeat numbers 3, 4, 6, and 7 until you reach the end of the row.

8. Cut the end of the knotting yarn at the bottom of the gauge.
9. a. If loops are desired, pull out the gauge.
   b. If a cut pile is desired, cut the knots at the bottom of the gauge.
10. Weave a few rows of plain weave before beginning another row of Ghiordes Knots. This helps to keep the knots in place.

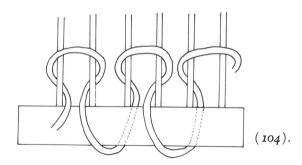

(*104*).

One, two, three or more colors can be used for each knot. The colors can be gradually, or quickly, changed from one area to the next. The colors may be the same or different from the warp.

The yarns can all be of one fiber, or different fibers can be mixed together. The size of the knot may vary from very short to very long. Rows of knots may overlap—or with more rows of plain weave between, just touch one another.

This is a technique worth experimenting with.

Weaving with Thick and Thin Wefts

Surprising effects can be achieved just by weaving with two shuttles wound with yarns of varying sizes. This is a pretty,

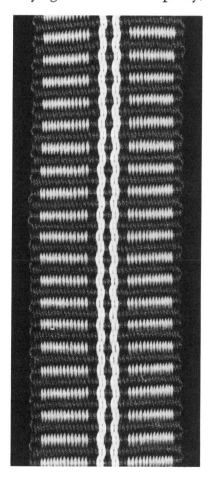

(*105*). Plain weave inkle band that forms the center of the Christmas trees in photographs (*106*) and (*107*). *Photograph—Seymour Bress.*

77

(106), (107). The heavy, rigid wefts used on alternate rows, distort the original "look" of the inkle band, photograph (105). See accompanying text for more details. *Photographs —Seymour Bress.*

though not spectacular band. In it there are almost equal amounts of black and red, and a touch of gold. These two trees were made on the same warp, and their center is now quite dramatic. The band in the tree on the left (illustration 106) is now predominantly red with a touch of gold and black. A heavy, rigid weft was used on the "red" shed. The one on the right (illustration 107) is predominantly black, with a touch of gold and red. A heavy rigid weft was used on the "black" shed. In the weaving of the trees, a fine weft thread was used throughout, but in every other shed, a heavy weft was used, too.

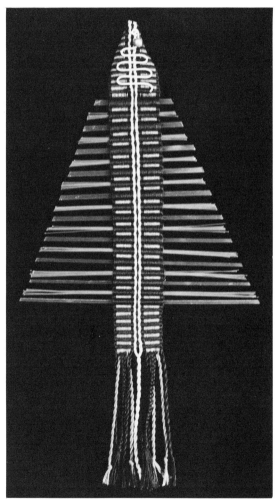

(106).

(107)

78

This technique shows up best when the contrast between weft yarns is great.

Use two shuttles. Wind one with fine weft yarn. Wind the other with very heavy weft yarn. (This may be several strands put together.)

TO WEAVE:

Weave one row with one shuttle.

Weave the next row with the other shuttle.

Alternate the two shuttles throughout.

The effect you get will look like this:

(*108*). Bright blue and Kelly green band woven with one heavy and one fine weft.

Because of the extra heavy weft, the selvedges will be wavy rather than straight. In many patterns, the back side will look quite different from the front side.

Another interesting way of weaving with two wefts of unequal size is to:

> Weave one row with heavy yarn
> Weave one row with fine yarn,

Repeat this 3 or more times, then

> Weave *another* row with *fine* yarn—one time.

Now go back to the beginning and start all over again.
The effect will be like this:

(*109*).

When weaving with weft materials of unequal sizes, such as
the plastic bars in the hanging in photograph 74, the effect is
still different and quite pronounced.

Beads and Bells

Beads are a delight! They come in all colors, shapes, sizes,
and materials. They can blend in with your piece—or be *just*
that accent it needs. They can be earthy or elegant. And they're
so available.

Hobby stores and dime stores sell them singly, but surely
you must know of other sources. How about that box of broken
jewelry in the top, middle drawer, or the necklaces in the
dime store, department stores, import houses, museum shops
and the like. Perhaps you have a potter friend who can make
some—or perhaps you'd like to try to make some yourself.

It is not possible to say exactly what shape and size your
beads should be. Of course, the holes in the beads must be big

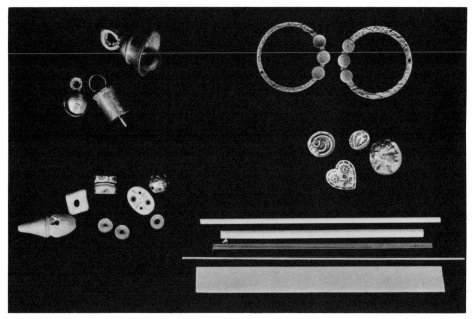

(*110a*). Beads, buttons, bells, rings and bars—interesting accessories to weave into inkle bands.

enough to fit onto the warp or weft thread. Beads will distort the woven area; small beads will distort the least, large ones the most. Clusters of beads will increase the distortion. This distortion becomes an interesting and integral part of the design.

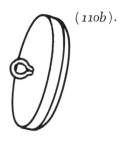

(*110b*).

Round beads can be used on either warp or weft. Long, tubular beads will probably best be accommodated on the warp. Buttons with shanks can be used on either warp or weft.

Beads can be slipped onto either the warp or weft yarns and pushed into place when wanted. Since there is usually a little less pre-planning when using them for weft, this is the method I favor.

It's very helpful to have a very simple sketch of your plan. In this way you'll remember what you had in mind when you strung those beads on! Something as simple as this will do.

(*111*).

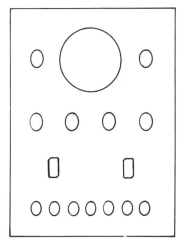

81

Before you start on your search for beads, let's see how they can be used in inkle weaving.

To use beads in the weft:

> Wind the shuttle with weft yarn.
>
> Decide how many beads you will use—and in what order. (If all the beads are the same size and color, the order doesn't matter.)
>
> Slip them onto the weft thread in *REVERSE* order. The last one on will be the first you will use.
>
> Push them along the weft thread for a distance so that they'll be out of the way until needed.
>
> Weave in the usual manner.

When a bead is desired:

> Open a shed.
>
> Bring the bead (or beads) along the weft and place it where you want it to show. Gently push it into place.
>
> Change sheds and beat.

The warp will spread above and below the bead a bit—more or less depending upon the size of the bead. When designing your band, you can minimize or exaggerate this space to advantage.

(*112*), (*113*), (*114*). Beads woven in. Details of hangings.

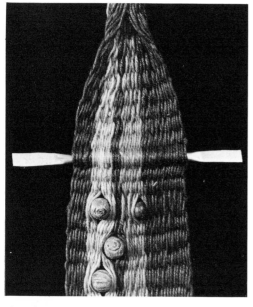 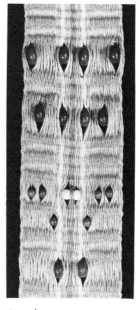 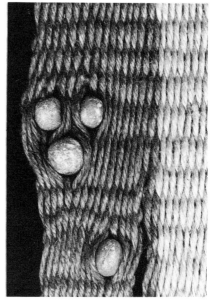

(*112*).   (*113*).   (*114*).

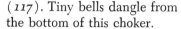
(115). Small glass beads woven into a gold lamé belt.

(116). Ceramic beads woven into a heavy linen belt.

(117). Tiny bells dangle from the bottom of this choker.

To Use Beads in the Warp

For explanation purposes, let's assume you are going to use beads on every warp thread.

Decide how many beads you will use, and in what order. (If all the beads are to be the same color and size, the order doesn't matter.)

Before securing your first warp thread, slip the beads onto it in *reverse* order of use.

Now, warp your first thread as usual.

Cut the thread at the front bar.

Onto the yarn that will form the second warp thread, slip some beads in reverse order of use.

Tie the 1st and 2nd warp threads together and continue to warp with the second thread.

Continue warping in this way. When the loom is completely warped, loosen the tension on the threads, and gently push the beads back beyond the heddles and the top bar. This will allow you to make a shed easily. Retension and weave.

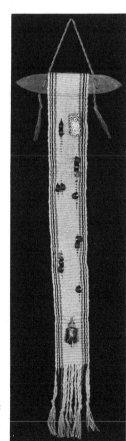

(118). Cottolin hanging. The African trade bead was put on the warp; the other beads and bell were woven in on the weft. *Photograph—Seymour Bress.*

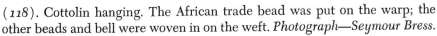

When you want to use a bead, bring it forward and put it in place. If the bead is on a heddle warp thread, you'll probably have to release the tension and baby it through the heddle.

Don't Forget—When advancing the warp, and the beads must go around any of the dowels on the loom, RELEASE THE TENSION GREATLY and gently ease the beads around the dowels.

One doesn't always plan ahead, and besides, special problems require special solutions.

This necklace, for example, was an afterthought (illustration 119). There was a little bit of warp left on the loom, and so it came into being. After deciding that the flat ceramic disc was to be the central point of interest, I had to decide how to get it on.

(*119*). Linen neckpiece with beads woven in on warp and weft.

(*120*). Close-up of photograph. See text for description of how the ceramic disc was woven in.

The disc is squat and heavy. If used on the weft thread, it would distort the weaving too much. I really wanted it to lie flat on top of the weaving.

The end of the warp was in sight. I eyed the row of knots that was nearing the top bar. I wondered if I could untie one of the knots in the center, slip the disc on, push it forward to the woven part, and then retie the warp threads. I tried it—and it worked. The disc was so heavy, though, that I really wanted some more warp threads in it for support. I untied two more warp threads, took them out of the heddles, and strung the bead onto them. I then put the threads back through their respective heddles, over the top bar, and tied them again.

The ceramic disc sits snugly on top of the woven part—and only we are the wiser.

Space-Dyed Yarns

It's fun to explore the potentials of different kinds of yarns. In the upper right hand corner of the basket of yarns on page 121, you'll see a skein of space-dyed yarns. It's a rather common yarn, but it can be handled in an unusual way in inkle weaving.

When you pull out a strand, you find that the color of it changes gradually, usually from light to dark. In the usual American-made space-dyed yarns, there are four color changes, and the colors change at regular intervals. If you just use this yarn as it comes from the skein—and make no attempt to control it at all—you might get an unusual effect, but it probably won't be very pretty. Since you know that the colors repeat at regular intervals, you can control this yarn to suit yourself. If you follow the description of the warping of the hanging that is pictured (illustration 121), you'll get an idea of how this works.

(121). Space-dyed yarns were used in a controlled way to achieve the effect in this hanging. Warping directions are in the text. Other information in Appendix. Shown in color on Plate 7.

(*122*). Draft for the space–dyed hanging in photograph (*121*).
(B = Royal Blue; S = Space–Dyed—white, pale green, olive green)

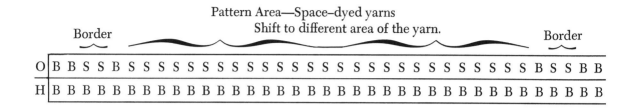

The first five threads were warped in the usual manner. So far, there is just one space-dyed yarn on the loom, and it's time for the second. It is *NOT* tied on randomly as it comes from the skein. The yarn is pulled out until the color sequence is at the same place as the first space-dyed yarn. At this point, it is tied onto the warp. The color changes should parallel the first rather closely as it goes around the loom.

After the next few solid blue threads are warped, a space-dyed yarn is used again. This time, however, the color sequence is shifted so that a different effect can be achieved. The first two space-dyed yarns started out light and gradually became darker; this space-dyed yarn will start with the dark area and gradually get lighter. The whole central portion was warped like this. The right border is a repeat of the left.

In other words, random use of space-dyed yarns results in a hodge-podge. However, if groups of space-dyed yarns follow the same sequence of colors together for a few times, a more cohesive effect results. Surrounding the space-dyed group of yarns with a solid color area adds a quieting effect.

It's almost impossible to line the space-dyed yarns up perfectly. Therefore, a little "bleeding" of colors from one color change to another will occur. Fortunately, this adds a nice quality to the weaving.

Some of the nicest bands I've made using this technique are with yarns which have gradual and close color changes. Unfortunately, subtlety doesn't show up too well in photographs.

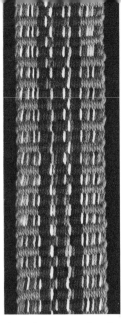

(123). Space–dyed yarns were used randomly in this belt.

(125). Space–dyed yarns were lined up to form little squares of colors. The colors on the right and left were lined up in the same way; the yarn was moved to a different position in the center, so that the sequence of colors would shift.

(124). Very softly shaded space–dyed wool yarn was used in this belt. The yarns were not lined up precisely, and the finished belt has a subtle, tie–dyed appearance.

(126). Baby sweaters are often made with the yarn used here. It is a solid color yarn with occasional spots of color. Although I attempted to line the spots up, the yarn was so springy that the spots would not line up throughout the warp.

(*127*). This space-dyed, loop mohair yarn from Holland would not be tamed. See text for details.

In the mail I received a delightful gift and a challenge from a good friend. It was a skein of space-dyed loop mohair yarn in colors ranging from purply red through red, orange and yellow. The label said that it was from Holland.

At first, I saw a double challenge: 1—loop mohair is tricky to use in inkle weaving, and 2—the colors, though brilliant and beautiful, are not ones I generally use.

Very soon I found a third challenge. I pulled out a long strand of the yarn—and could not find any place where the color order repeated itself!

My solution to the challenges were these:

1. I used the loop mohair yarn in just two small areas, and kept them on the "Open" threads.
2. I chose a solid purple wool yarn to surround the multicolored areas, and added just a touch of black wool in the center.
3. Because there were no color pattern repeats, and there were so many color changes, I used the mohair just as it came from the skein.

The effect was pretty. It's a bit unusual—yet not startling.

Basically, I think that you get best results with space-dyed yarns if you

align the colors

use them in concentrated areas

surround them with solid color areas.

Tie Dye

When working with commercial space-dyed yarns, you're limited in color and pattern designing by the yarns that are available. But—you can dye-it-yourself—and get some fascinating results.

When yarn is tie-dyed, sections of yarn are dyed at a time. Those that are not being dyed are tied, wrapped or held in some way so that the dye doesn't penetrate the yarn. Important details about this art can be found in books listed in the bibliography.

As you know, it's the warp threads in inkle weaving that form the pattern. Therefore, it's those threads that will have to be dyed. Here are some types of patterns that can be achieved by tie-dyeing warp threads.

1. Horizontal stripes

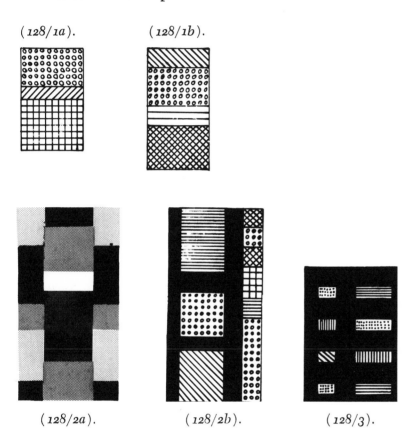

(*128/1a*).   (*128/1b*).

(*128/2a*).   (*128/2b*).   (*128/3*).

2. Vertical stripes
3. Vertical stripes tie-dyed on one shed, solid color on the other.
4. Solid color band—with small section of tie-dyed warp.

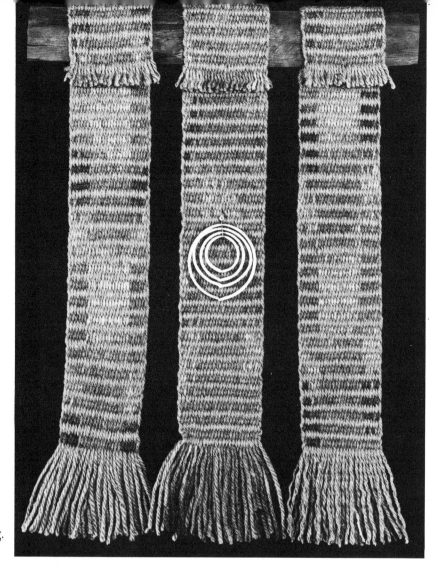

(*129*). Tie-dyed wall hanging. Shown in color on Plate 4.

Here are some very general directions for tie-dyeing your warp.

1. Determine how long you want your warp to be. To this figure, add a few inches for shrinkage.
2. Decide how many threads will be in each section of your design.
3. Measure off the number of threads you need for a complete section of your design. Have each thread the length determined in step 1.

The measuring may be done on the inkle loom, a warping frame, or any contrived device.

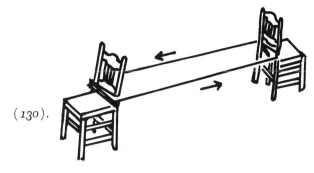

(130).

It's easiest if the threads are continuous and not cut until they're ready to be used.

    4. Tie the threads together—loosely—in several places. Handle the "skein" you've made gently, so that the threads don't move around too much.

You're ready to tie-dye your warp threads now—and the fun begins. Unfortunately, I can't give you directions here. The particular yarns and dye you are using and the type of pattern you are making will determine how you proceed.

Your first attempt may or may not come out precisely as planned. Be gentle with yourself. It's well known that there's a bit of magic in every dye pot. Flexibility is needed. It may not be exactly what you intended, but surely you can arrange it to look well, anyhow.

With a little experience, you can get random, controlled, symmetrical, asymmetrical, and geometric patterns. And when you get super-skilled, you can even do pictorial patterns.

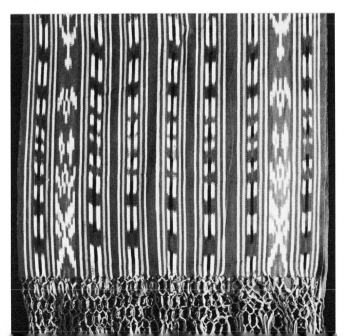

(131). Elaborate tie-dyed shawl from Ecuador. Although this was *not* woven on an inkle loom, the patterns are almost completely warp-faced and can be used for inkle weaving. *Courtesy—Katherine Driver. Photograph—Seymour Bress.*

(132). Some very skillful Guatemalan people tie-dyed the yarn for this warp-faced shawl. No, it wasn't woven on an inkle loom, but it is an adaptable idea. *Courtesy— Katherine Driver. Photograph —Seymour Bress.*

(133). Close–up of the flower and people figures.

Shaping a Piece

There are times when you may want to alter the shape of your band. There are a few ways that you can do this.

When possible, start with the widest part first. The simplest way to narrow it down, is to draw the weft a bit tighter, row after row, until the band is the width you want. When you want it wider again, gradually loosen up on the weft thread. The narrower part will be stiffer than the wider part.

(134).

If you want the feel of the finished piece to remain the same throughout, then try this method of narrowing:

> Weave full width in the usual manner until you want to narrow your band.
>
> Put the shuttle into the next shed as usual, but withdraw it from the shed, one, two, or more threads before the selvedge.
>
> Change sheds and beat.
>
> Put the shuttle in where you withdrew it before, and weave up to the last few edge threads.
>
> Withdraw your shuttle before you reach the edge threads.
>
> Continue to narrow down in this way until you reach the width you want.

(135).

For a gradual narrowing, omit the threads 1 or 2 at a time. For a more sudden change, omit more threads at one time.

DO NOT CUT the warp threads if you are going to widen the band later on.

To widen again, just weave over more and more of the dropped selvedge threads, until the band is the width you want. When the piece is finished, the loose warp ends can be cut and darned back in.

As you eliminate edge threads from the weaving, what happens to the pattern on the band? Well, unless there are broad, solid stripes on either side, it changes quite a bit. Take this into consideration when planning your design.

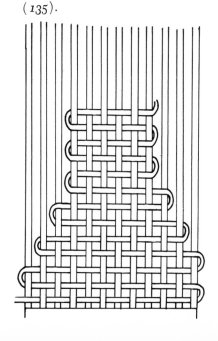

93

Yes, if you want to add warp threads, you can do that, too. You'll need to put some heddles on the loom where the new warp threads are to go. Cut the new warp threads the length of your unfinished warp ends—plus about six inches. Attach (knot or pin) the new warp ends at the end of the warp, and bring them around in proper order—heddle and open—to the woven part. Keep them taut, and pin them down, one by one, to the woven part of the band. Now you're ready to weave over these new threads. The loose ends can be darned back into the finished band later on.

Generally, neckties are shaped, but their particular shape varies from time to time. A current necktie pattern will be a good guide for you as you are weaving.

A little spice can be added to belts, necklaces and bracelets by shaping them. With wall hangings, of course, there is free rein.

Loops

Here's another simple and effective technique to add to your inkle weaving vocabulary. With loops, you can get an effective textural change, color change, and can even vary your pattern a bit.

A small, round, pointed tool is needed for this. A knitting needle, pointed dowel, pencil, or chopstick will work well.

Two weft threads are recommended. One should be the same color as the edge threads of the warp. This one will not show. The other can be any color or texture desired—and will be pulled up into loops that will show on the surface.

To Weave:

> Weave a few rows of plain weave with both the binder weft and the weft yarn for the loops. This is just to secure the "loop" yarn in well. End with the wefts on the right side.
>
> Change sheds and beat.
>
> Put the "loop" weft into this shed. Let it lie loosely there.

94

Decide where you want your loops to be.

Starting from the right side, separate the two warp threads where the first loop will show.

With the pointed stick, reach in between these warp threads and loop the weft yarn around the stick.

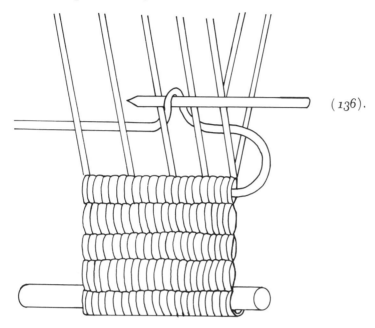

(136).

Withdraw the stick from the shed and bring it to the spot where the next loop is desired.

Repeat the process across the row.

The pointed stick is now lying on top of the warp threads and the loops are lined up on it.

Into this same shed, put the binder weft.

Change sheds and beat.

Withdraw the pointed stick.

Repeat this process wherever loops are desired.

If you are going to have loops on the next row, they will have to be picked up from left to right. If you are right-handed, you will probably find this rather awkward. Perhaps it would help if you reached in for the weft thread with the fingers of your right hand—or a crochet hook, and then slipped the weft onto the pointed stick.

The loops are not as secure as the Ghiordes knot, but they are packed in very firmly and should be quite durable. You have much design freedom with loops. They can be used with a patterned or solid colored warp. On a solid color warp, they could easily be combined with other techniques such as brocade.

(*137*). Bolivian fabric with loops forming the design. The idea is adaptable to inkle bands. *Courtesy—Katherine Driver. Photograph—Seymour Bress.*

VI. *Pick It Up*

Pick-Up Techniques

Delightful designs can be made using any of several pick-up techniques. Design possibilities range from simple geometric designs to elaborate animal and humanistic figures. The techniques are all rather easy to do—but are much slower than plain weave. After looking at some of the finished patterns, I think you'll agree that they're worth a little extra time.

In plain weave, you open each shed and weave completely across the row. There is no manipulation of threads. In the pick-up techniques, threads *are* manipulated. In brocade, one of the two weft threads goes part way through the shed, is brought to the surface, goes over a few warp threads and then disappears again in the shed. In other types of pick-up, some warp threads are either picked up from the bottom shed, or pushed down from the top, according to the design desired.

Each type of pick-up has its own threading, method of working, and weights of yarns that work best for it; each has its own "look." In all, the background is repetitive and usually flat, while the pattern threads on the foreground are slightly raised, bold, or contrasting in color to the background.

As complex as the pick-up techniques may appear, they are really quite easy to do. We'll explore four of these techniques.

(*138*). Brocade sampler.

97

Brocade

Brocade is the only technique where the *weft* plays an important part in the pattern. The pattern weft floats on top of the warp threads to form the design.

There are many different ways to do brocade. Here's one specific way now, and later I'll suggest ways to vary this.

(*139*). Draft for brocade.

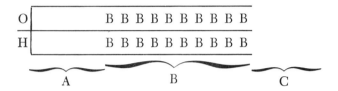

A & C—Borders as desired.
B—Pattern Area—all threads same color and weight.

YARNS NEEDED:

Warp—relatively smooth and light-weight yarns. Some good choices are perle cotton 5/2, crochet cotton standard weight, or fine linen.

Except for the border, all the warp threads are usually the same color and weight.

Weft—two weft threads are needed:

1. Binder weft—same weight and color as the edge warp threads.
2. Pattern weft—heavier and fluffier yarn than the warp. Contrasting color to warp.

Some good choices:

Floss—doubled if necessary
Wools

How to Weave:

Open a shed.

1. In this shed, weave all across with both binder and pattern threads. This secures both threads.

98

2. Change sheds and beat firmly.
3. Weave all across with the binder weft.
4. Hold the top layer of threads in your left hand.

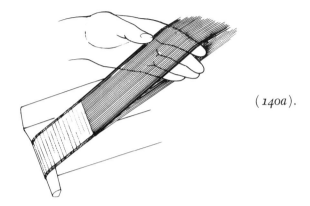

(*140a*).

5. Insert the pick-up stick into this shed, from right to left.

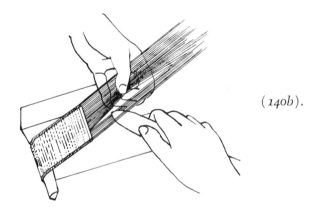

(*140b*).

6. Transfer the threads from the top layer onto the pick-up stick until you reach the place where the design begins.
7. Bring the pick-up stick to the surface, on top of the warp threads that will be covered by the design, and then back into the shed.
   Repeat this across the row wherever the pattern is to show.

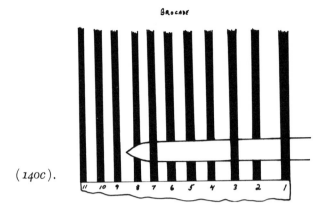

(140c).

8. Turn the pick-up stick on edge. This creates a **shed** for the pattern weft.

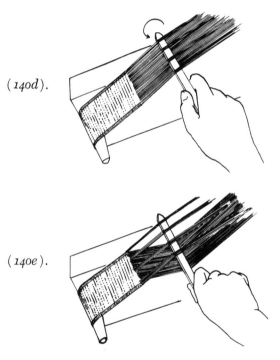

(140d).

(140e).

9. Weave across the row with the pattern weft. Remove the pick-up stick.
10. Change sheds and beat firmly.

Repeat steps 3–10 for each pattern row.

In this method, the pattern threads are seen on the front only.

Floats

The pattern is formed by *weft* floats. Under most circumstances, it would be undesirable to have these floats more than ¼ inch long. If the pattern calls for a longer float, you can break it up and tie it down occasionally with a warp thread. This "tie-down" can add interest to the pattern if it is done in an orderly way for each line. Notice the tie downs on the figures in photographs 141, 142 and 143.

(*141*). Scores of brocaded animals adorn this fabric which was woven in Mexico. Notice the tie-down threads. *Photograph—Seymour Bress.*

(*142*). Brocade birds. *Photograph—Seymour Bress.*

(*143*). Geometric, brocaded designs done on a backstrap loom in Guatemala. *Photograph—Seymour Bress.*

Background

The background for brocade is usually a solid color and is completely unobtrusive.

Types of Patterns

All kinds of designs are appropriate for brocade—geometric designs, people figures, flowers, animals. The more warp threads, the more elaborate the design can be. Keep in mind that the finer the warp threads, the more threads per inch there will be.

(*144*). Brocaded scrap salvaged from a well-worn purse. Floats are rather long, and many straggly threads have been snipped. Woven in Mexico. *Photograph—Seymour Bress.*

(145).   (146).

(147).   (148).

(145), (146), (147), (148).
Close-ups of brocaded figures.
These were woven on a backstrap loom in Guatemala. The
figures will adapt well for
inkle weaving.

103

The designs can be improvised directly on the loom, or drawn out on graph paper and followed from this.

The warp threads in one row are not *directly* above the warp threads in the next. They are over to the side—just a bit. Therefore, a straight line on graph paper will be a slightly jagged line on the woven piece. Remember this when translating your pattern idea to the loom.

Once you understand the general idea behind brocade, you can vary the instructions in many ways.

For one thing, the pattern weft doesn't have to go from edge to edge. It can be inserted as desired and stopped when no longer needed. Also, two or more colors can be used in one row.

When you have a pattern in a small area, the pattern will have little curves at the edges where it goes from one row to the next.

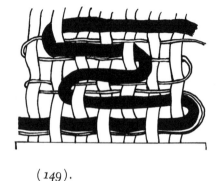

(149).

(149a).   (149b).

(149c).

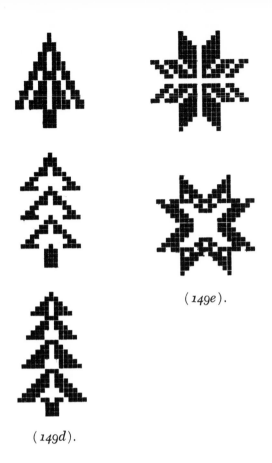

(*149e*).

(*149d*).

If you don't want these curves to show, you can drop the pattern weft to the underside when you are finished with it for that row. Then, change sheds and bring it up again where desired.

You might like to use some beads, or make some loops or Ghiordes knots with your brocaded piece. They will combine quite well.

Basketweave Background

This technique has been used quite extensively in the Scandinavian countries as well as other European countries. Some of the most beautiful and elaborate designs have been done on this threading.

(*150*). Hanging. Seven pick-up designs with basketweave background were done on one warp. They are displayed on a sawed-down boomerang.

(*151*). Common draft for all basketweave background pick-up patterns.

O	F			F F H F F H F F H F		F
H	F			F H F F H F F H F F		F

A   B   C

F—Fine; H—Heavy
A & C—Borders as desired, but the edge threads should
be the same color as the fine background threads
B—Patterns area—repeat as often as desired—F,F,H

THREADS TO USE:

Background thread—fine
Pattern thread—heavier and soft or fluffy

106

Some good combinations:

Warp: Background: Perle 5   Perle 3
         Pattern: Floss, Doubled   Knitting Worsted
Weft: Same color and weight as the background thread.
         It is pretty when doubled.

When woven in plain weave, an attractive spotted pattern appears. The pattern threads form the spots, and the spots alternate from row to row. If you look at the draft, you'll see why this happens.

It is interesting to note that if the pattern threads were completely removed, and you wove in plain weave, the effect would be sort of a "basket" weave.

If the weft were doubled, it would be a true basket weave.

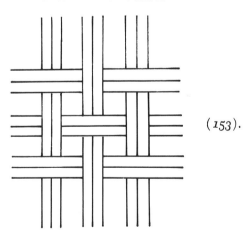

(*153*).

Can you see why this basket weave forms? If you eliminate the heavy pattern threads from the draft, you would have two "heddle" threads side by side, and two "open" threads side by side, all across the pattern area. Therefore, when you weave, you would go over and under pairs of threads. With a doubled weft, this makes a basket weave. Because of this pairing, by the way, the weft *does* show.

When you do the pick-up pattern, the heavy pattern threads float under or over the surface—and the resulting background is this basket weave.

The design is made by warp pattern thread floats. Usually, it is undesirable to have floats of more than 3 or 4 threads. This limits your design possibilities. It's surprising though, the great diversity that can be achieved within this limitation.

The theory behind this pick-up technique is very simple. When you're weaving, and you *don't* want a pattern thread to show, you either leave it on the bottom, if it's there—or push it to the bottom if it's on the top. You then weave over it.

If you *want* a pattern thread to show and it's on the top— leave it there. If it's on the bottom, reach down and bring it to the top. Keep it up—and weave under it.

Now, for specific directions:

For a Solid Background, with No Pattern Threads Showing:

> Raise a shed.
> Hold the top layer in your left hand.
> Insert your pick-up stick into this shed from right to left.
> Transfer the threads from your left hand onto the pick-up stick until you reach the first pattern thread.
> Place the pattern thread *under* the pick-up stick.

(154a).

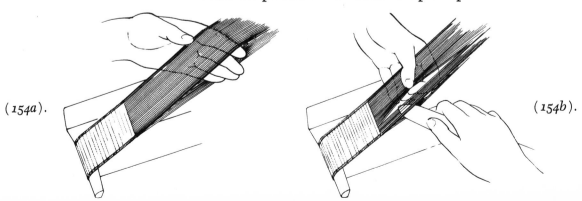

(154b).

Repeat the previous two steps all across the row.

(154c).

Turn the pick-up stick on edge and weave through the shed you've made.

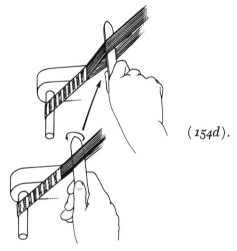

(154d).

Change sheds, beat, and repeat the same procedure.

For a Solid Pattern Area with No Background Showing:

Raise a shed.
Hold the top layer with your left hand.
Insert your pick-up stick into this shed from right to left.
Now you want the pattern threads from both layers to be ON THE TOP layer.

Transfer the threads from your left hand onto the pick-up stick until you reach the first pattern thread that is on the bottom layer.

Reach down with the pick-up stick and put the pattern thread ON TOP of the pick-up stick. Be sure that the pattern thread is brought up between the two warp threads that are warped to either side of it. Do this all across the row.

(154e).

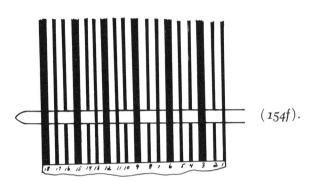

(154f).

Turn the pick-up stick on edge.

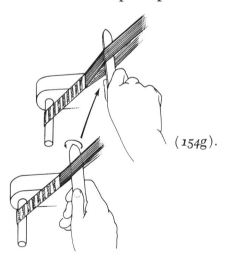

(154g).

Weave through the shed you've made.
Change sheds, beat, and repeat this same process.

To Weave a Pattern with a Solid Background:

> Raise a shed.
>
> Hold the top layer with your left hand.
>
> Insert the pick-up stick into this shed from right to left.
>
> Transfer the threads from your left hand onto the pick-up stick. Pick up the pattern threads you want for your design from the bottom layer and put them ON TOP of the stick
>
> and
>
>> Put the pattern threads that are not to show in the design, UNDER the stick.
>
> Turn the pick-up stick on edge.
>
> Weave across the row through the shed you've made.
>
> Change sheds—and repeat this procedure with your next design row.

To Weave a Pattern with a Spotted Background:

> Raise a shed.
>
> Hold the top layer with your left hand.
>
> Insert your pick-up stick into this shed from right to left.
>
> Transfer the threads from your left hand onto the pick-up stick. Leave all the pattern threads from the top layer, ON TOP of the pick-up stick,
>
> and
>
>> Reach down to the bottom layer with the pick-up stick and put any pattern thread that belongs in this row of your design, ON TOP of the pick-up stick, too.

No pattern threads from the top layer are put under the pick-up stick.

> Turn the pick-up stick on edge.
>
> Weave through the shed you've made.
>
> Change sheds, beat, and continue in the same way.

When you feel adventurous, both backgrounds can be combined well in one piece.

111

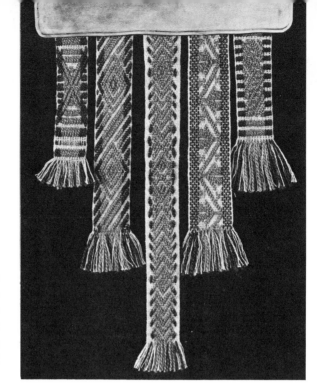

(155). Hanging with leather heading. Five different patterns were tried out on one warp. The sections were cut apart, mounted on a thin board and faced with a leather topping.

(156). Doramay Keasbey became intrigued with the basketweave background pick-up technique, and designed and wove many patterns for it. Photographs (156–166) are close-ups from a belt she wove to wear with a folk dancing costume.

(157).

(158).

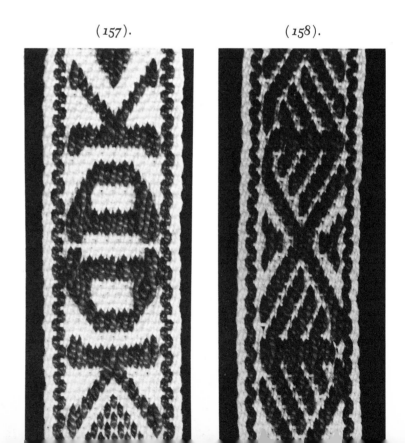

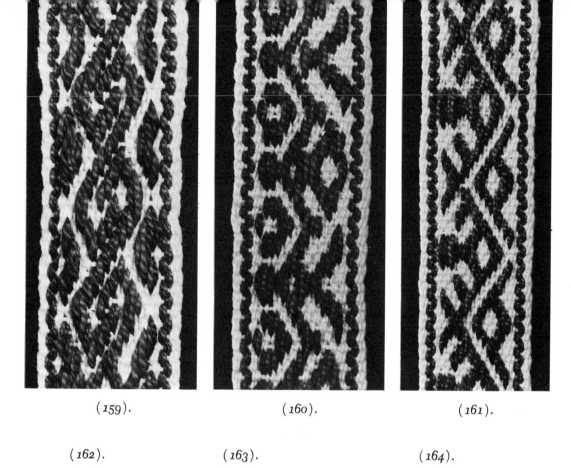

(159).   (160).   (161).

(162).   (163).   (164).

(165).   (166).   (167).

(168).   (169).   (170).

($167–180$). Pick-up patterns with basketweave background.

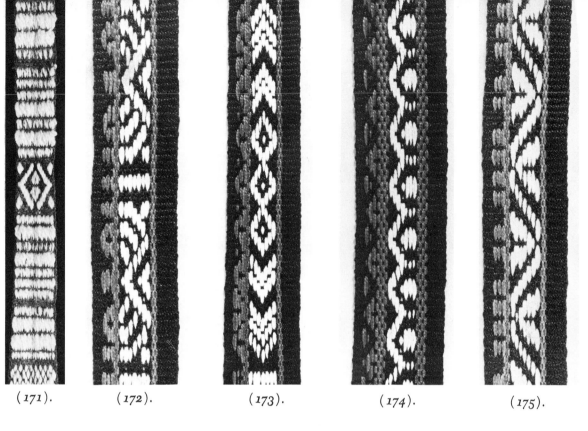

(171).   (172).   (173).   (174).   (175).

(176).

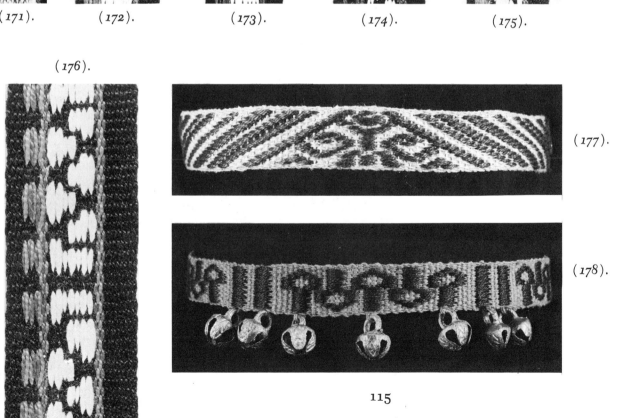

(177).

(178).

115

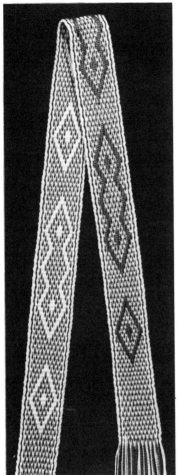

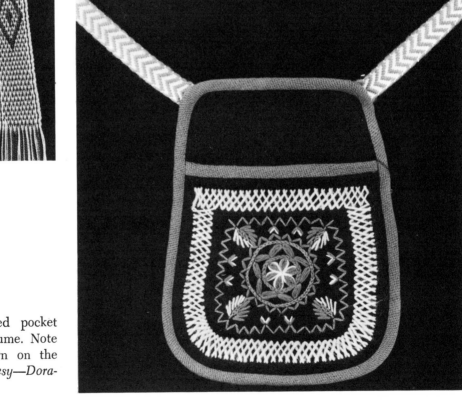

(179).

(180).

(181). Embroidered pocket for a Finnish costume. Note the pick-up pattern on the waistband. *Courtesy—Doramay Keasbey.*

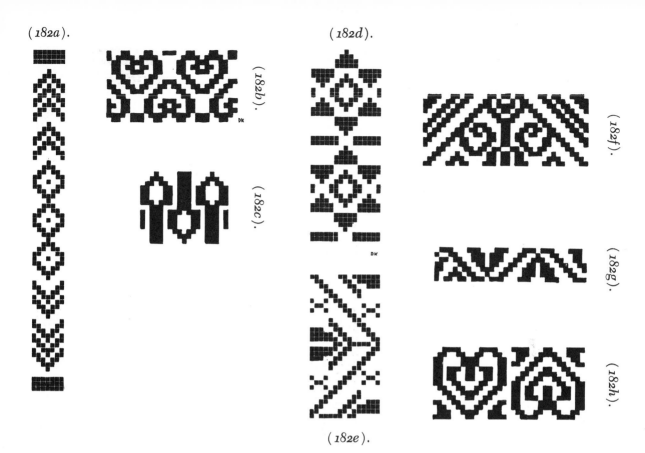

(182a).

(182d).

(182b).

(182c).

(182f).

(182g).

(182h).

(182e).

Horizontal Stripe Background

This is a simple and popular technique, and many interesting patterns can be made with it. The background of horizontal bars is its distinguishing characteristic.

(183a). Geometric pick-up pattern with horizontal stripe background.

117

(*183b*). Common draft for bands using horizontal stripe background technique.
D = Dark; L = Light

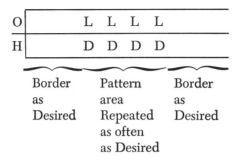

O	L L L L
H	D D D D

Border	Pattern	Border
as	area	as
Desired	Repeated	Desired
	as often	
	as Desired	

THREADS NEEDED:

Warp—

Background thread—any thread, same grist or slightly finer than the pattern thread. Contrasting color to pattern thread.

Pattern thread—same grist or slightly heavier than background thread. Contrasting color to background thread.

Some possibilities—

Cottons work quite well;

Perle cotton #5—light background

Floss   —slightly heavier pattern thread

Weft—

The weft does not show. It should be the same color as the selvedge threads. The weight is usually the same as the warp or doubled.

When plain weave is woven, one row is a solid light color, and the other is a solid dark color in the pattern area, forming horizontal stripes. These stripes are always more or less visible in the pattern area. The pattern is formed with warp floats, and the floats never exceed three threads. The floats in one pattern row always alternate with the floats in the next pattern row. Unless the pattern progresses on a diagonal, the pattern area doesn't have a sharply defined edge, but staggers in and out slightly.

118

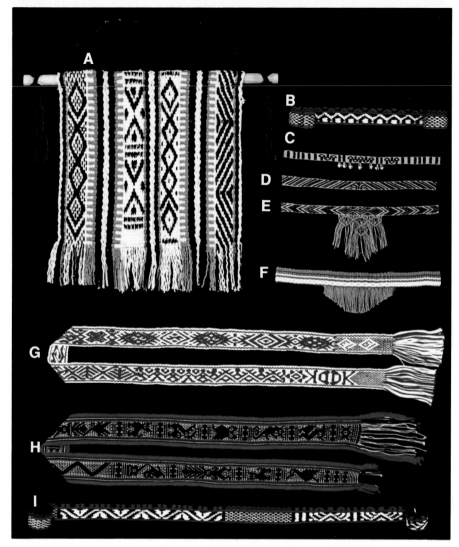

Plate 1

A. Except for the background, the patterns in the 1st & 3rd strips of this sampler are almost identical. Basketweave background pick-up technique.

B. Red on the asymmetric borders, black and white in-between. Design in basketweave background pick-up technique.

C. Bells edge this narrow choker. Pattern done in basketweave background pick-up technique.

D. A motif from a Russian carpet was the inspiration for the design on this choker. Basketweave background pick-up technique.

E. Long fringes were woven on one side of this necklace. When taken off the loom, some decorative knots and some tiny beads were added. Macramé and inkle weaving — an interesting combination.

F. A simple band with a shaped fringe.

G. One day Doramay Keasbey learned how to do basketweave background pick-up technique — and the next week she designed and wove this belt!
Artist — Doramay Keasbey

H. From Mexico comes this colorful belt — and it's filled with charming folk motifs. Speckled background pick-up technique.

Artist unknown.

I. Two more variations on a black, red, and white warp. Basketweave background pick-up technique.

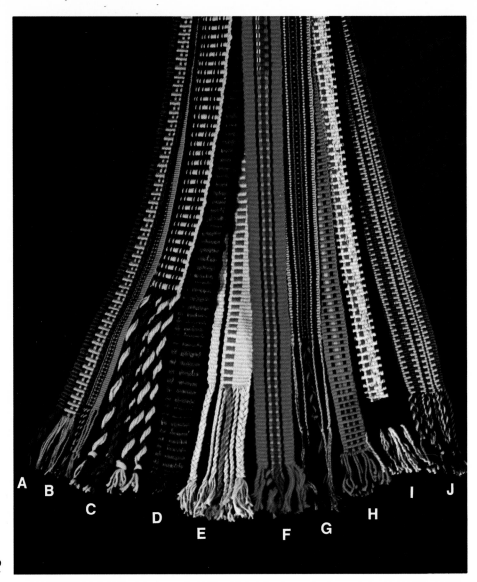

Plate 2

Left to Right:

A. Perle cotton in shades of green.

B. Crochet cotton and twisted ends.

C. Computer designed belt with long twisted ends. Acrylic rug yarn.

Weaver: Dan Bress

D. Blue and green Acrylic yarn — two wefts used — one thick, one thin.

E. Heavy rug wool used for this.

F. Acrylic, knitting worsted weight yarn for this one.

G. Pretty to look at — but difficult to weave. Fine nylon yarn.

H. Space-dyed acrylic yarns used in a controlled way.

I. Wrapped fringes on an acrylic, plain woven band.

J. Same yarn, same colors — but a different pattern from the first band (A).

Left to Right:

Except for F & G, all these bands are woven in plain weave.

A. Ladder-like design in rayon and linen yarn.

B. Textured yarns used here.

C. Gold linen combined with carved ceramic beads.

D. Handspun, vegetable dyed yarns.

E. Cotton Band.

F. Knitting worsted weight acrylic yarn, with a bulkier white yarn for accent. Fine weft is used and a simple pick-up pattern made after several rows of plain weaving. Technique: combination of plain weave and horizontal stripe background pick-up.

G. Mondrian-like pattern. Horizontal stripe background pick-up technique.

H. Interesting, subtly-colored acrylic yarns used here.

I. Nubby cotton and linen yarns — capped with a tassel.

J. Heavy weft used in this plain weave version of its twin, band (F).

Plate 3

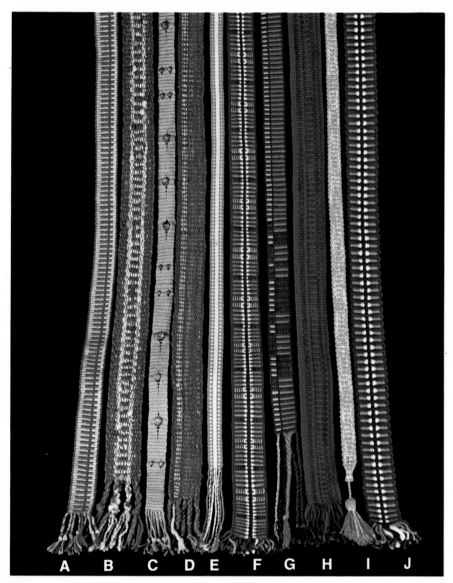

A B C D E F G H I J

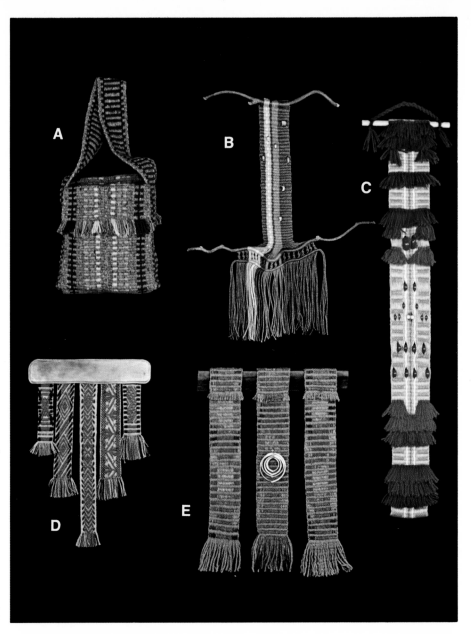

Plate 4

A. For the body of this purse, one strip was woven. It was cut in half, the pieces were put side by side and stitched together. A second strip was used for the handle. Acrylic, knitting worsted weight yarns.

B. Grape vines need to be pruned periodically. The vines are fun to weave with! A bit of macramé was added below the bottom vine.

C. Ghiordes knots and big and little beads adorn this linen and wool wall hanging.

D. A leather strip binds these pick-up samples together. Strips are in basketweave background pick-up technique.

E. Tie-dyed strips mounted on a chunky rosewood heading.

A. I always knew that this boomerang would come in handy! The ends were cut off and these strips were stapled onto it. Patterns are in the basketweave background pick-up technique.

B. By leaving the warp unwoven in areas, interesting effects can be achieved.

C. Brocaded bird sampler woven in 1962. Macramé fringe and topping added later.

D. There was just enough yarn left on a long linen warp to eke out this neckpiece. Beads were used in the warp and weft, and tabs were created at the bottom.

E. Put a feather in your cap—or headband—or whatever you will.

Plate 5

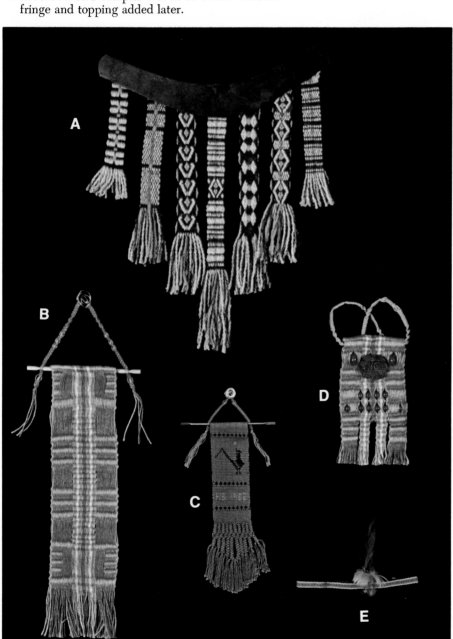

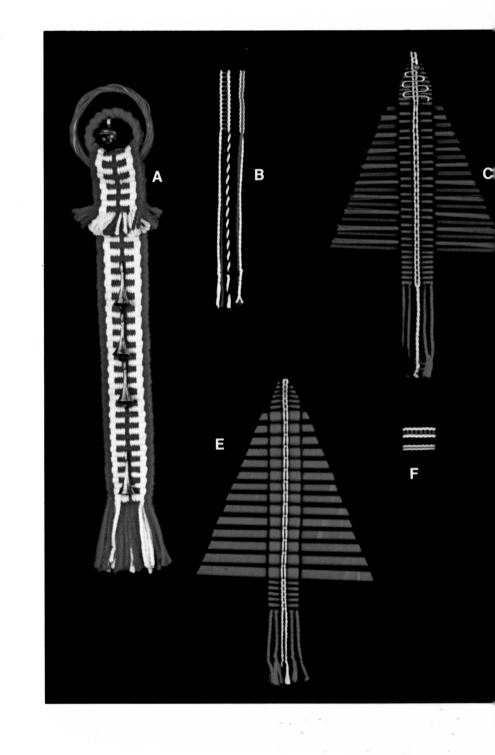

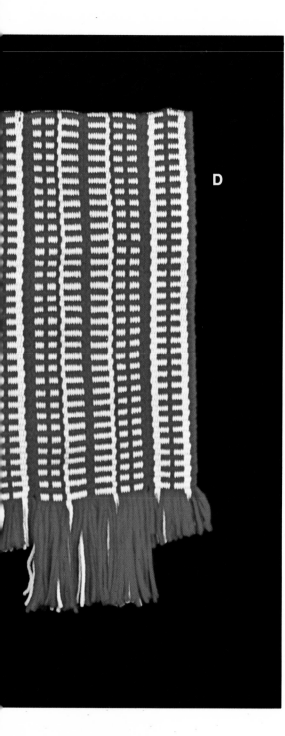

D

Plate 6

GIVE THESE AS GIFTS — OR DECO-
RATE YOUR OWN HOME.

A. Bell pull — Red and white acrylic yarns with long bells woven in.

B. End of belt showing the decorative finishing touches.

C. Plastic bars and rods were used as weft for this tree. They were carefully trimmed off the loom.

D. Cheerful and practical — this runner is made with acrylic yarns and is quite washable.

E. Although this tree was woven on the same warp as (C), the look of it is a bit different. The heavy rods were placed in the red shed for this tree and a fine weft was used for the black shed. In (C), the reverse order was used.

F. Here's a napkin ring woven with perle cotton. Designed and woven by Allen Bress.

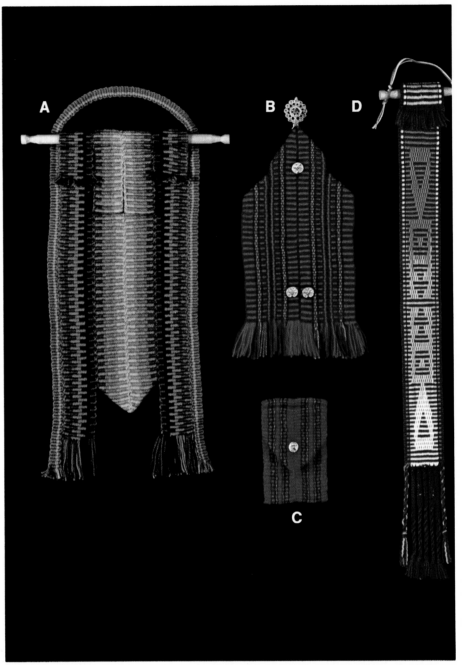

Plate 7

A. Dan Bress wove the strips for this hanging. I made just one cut before stitching them together.

B. Just one strip, only one — was used to make this hanging. Martha Hoering dyed the woolen yarns, I designed the piece, and Dan Bress wove it.

C. Purse with a thousand uses. A belt fits through the hem.

D. The color changes in this hanging were achieved by using space-dyed yarns in a controlled manner. Horizontal background pick-up technique used for the pattern.

How to Weave the Background

The background just forms naturally as you do plain weave.

The background can be the dark color and the pattern done with the light color or vice versa. To make it as clear as possible, I'll describe each way separately.

The two methods can be interchanged within the same piece.

To Weave—The Light Color Forming the Pattern:

Raise the light colored shed, beat, and weave all across.

Raise the dark colored shed. Beat.

Hold the top layer with your left hand.

Insert the pick-up stick into the shed from right to left.

Transfer the threads from your left hand to the pick-up stick until you reach the first pattern thread that will show in the design you've chosen. (The pattern thread will be on the bottom layer.)

Reach down to the bottom layer and slip the pattern thread onto the pick-up stick. Make sure that the pattern thread lies between the two threads directly above it.

Continue in this way across the row, picking up EVERY OTHER THREAD or ALTERNATE threads in the design area.

Turn the pick-up stick on edge.

Weave across the shed you've made.

(184a).

Change sheds and beat. The light colored shed is now up.

Weave across the row. No pick-up on this row.

Change sheds and beat. The dark colored shed is now up again.

Follow the direction as before, but this time pick up the threads in your design area which hadn't been picked up before. If the previous picked-up threads were even numbered threads, then these will be the odd numbered threads. The new picked up threads will never be directly above the picked-up pattern threads in the previous row—but rather over to either side of them.

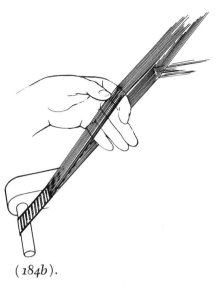

(184b).

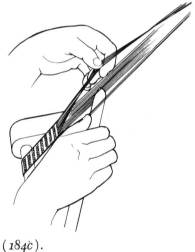

(184c).

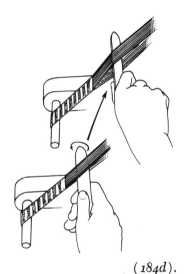

(184d).

To Weave—The Dark Color Forming the Pattern:

Raise the dark colored shed, beat, and weave all across.
Raise the light colored shed. Beat.
Hold the top layer with your left hand.
Insert the pick-up stick into the shed from right to left.
Transfer the threads from your left hand to the pick-up

stick until you reach the first pattern thread that will show in the design you've chosen. (The pattern thread will be on the bottom layer.)

Reach down to the bottom layer and slip the pattern thread onto the pick-up stick. Make sure that the pattern thread lies between the two threads directly above it.

Continue in this way across the row, picking up EVERY OTHER THREAD or ALTERNATE threads in the design area.

Turn the pick-up stick on edge.

Weave across the shed you've made.

Change sheds and beat. The dark-colored shed is now up.

Weave across the row. No pick-up on this row.

Change sheds and beat. The light-colored shed is now up again.

Follow the directions as before, but this time pick up the threads in your design area which hadn't been picked up before. If the previous picked up threads were even-numbered threads, then these will be the odd-numbered threads. The new picked-up threads will never be directly above picked-up pattern threads in the previous row, but rather to either side of them.

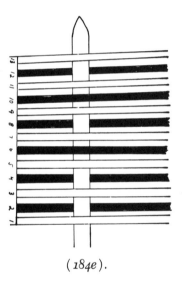

(184e).

Briefly:

When the light thread forms the pattern:

Raise the light-colored shed and weave all across.

Raise the dark-colored shed. Reach into the bottom layer and pick up *every other* thread in your design area.

Weave across.

Raise the light-colored shed and weave all across.

Raise the dark-colored shed. Reach into the bottom layer and pick up every other thread in your design area, making sure that they alternate with the previous pick-up threads.

Weave across.

121

When the dark thread forms the pattern:

Raise the dark-colored shed and weave all across.

Raise the light-colored shed. Reach into the bottom layer and pick up *every other* thread in your design area.

Weave across.

Raise the dark-colored shed and weave all across.

Raise the light-colored shed. Reach into the bottom layer and pick up *every other* thread in your design area, making sure that they alternate with the previous pick-up threads.

Weave across.

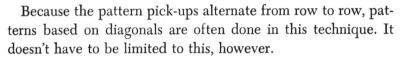

(185). Belt woven with traditional motifs. *Sylvia Pocock—weaver.*

Because the pattern pick-ups alternate from row to row, patterns based on diagonals are often done in this technique. It doesn't have to be limited to this, however.

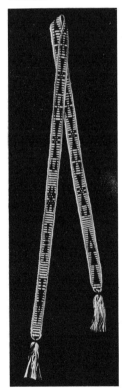

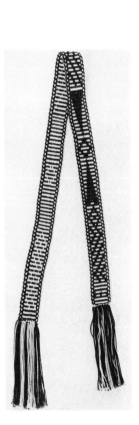

(186). *Susan Easton designed and wove this belt.*

(187). *Pattern designed by Susan Easton.*

(188). LEFT: Simple, asymmetric block pattern.

(189). When woven in plain weave, the band in photograph (188) looks like this. Three colors are used.

(190). When woven in plain weave with a heavy weft, the band in photograph (191) looks like this. The two white threads, on either side of the center, are extra heavy, bulky threads.

(191). With a finer weft, and occasional pick-ups, first on the light shed, then on the dark, a unique pattern emerges.

(192). A pattern based on a Peruvian design was woven on a space-dyed warp. See color plate 7D.

(193). Foreshortened version of pattern woven in photograph (192).

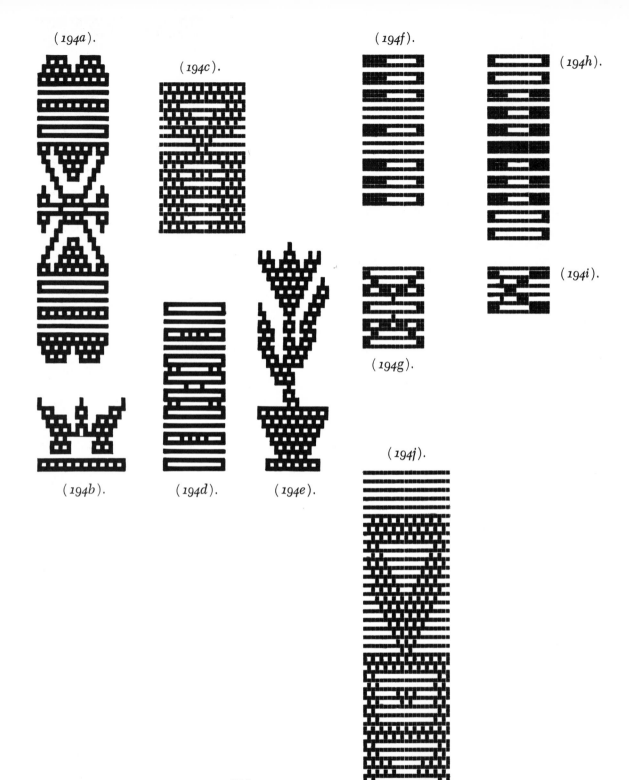

(194a).

(194c).

(194f).

(194h).

(194i).

(194g).

(194b).

(194d).

(194e).

(194j).

Speckled Background

This pick-up technique is unique because of the interesting speckled background that is formed throughout. Many Mexican, Ecuadorian, and Guatemalan belts are woven in this way. The range of designs that can be woven on a narrow fabric is enormous.

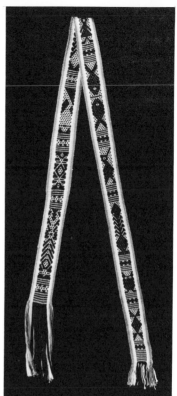

(197).

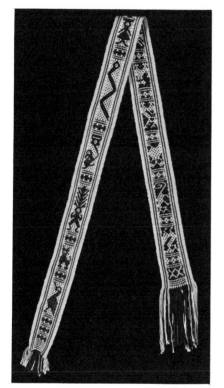

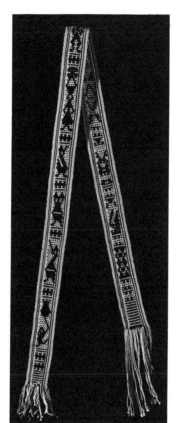

(196).

(195),/(196), (197), (198). Native Mexican belts. Front and under sides are shown. At the end of this section, close-ups of many of these delightful designs are shown.

(198).

125

The draft for this is the same as that for the horizontal stripe background pick-up technique, but the weights of the yarns differ.

(*199*). Common draft for bands using the speckled background pick-up technique.

F = Fine; H = Heavy

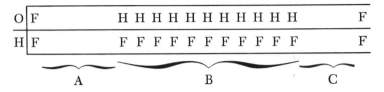

A & C = Borders as desired, but edge threads should be the same color as the fine background threads.

B = Pattern area—repeat as often as desired.

WARP:

For the pattern area, a fine thread and a very heavy thread are alternated. The selvedge threads should be the same color as the fine background thread in the design area. The colors should be contrasting. One possible combination is:

Perle cotton #5—one color

Rug yarn—contrasting color

WEFT:

The weft is the same as the fine warp thread. It *will* be visible, but should remain unobtrusive. Therefore, it should be the same color as the fine warp thread in the design area.

FLOATS:

Warp floats form the pattern in this weave. They are almost always three rows high. The floats alternate in brick-like fashion. Because of this, solid looking areas are built up, and patterns can be quite long.

BACKGROUND:

The background is speckled throughout. The spots on one row alternate with the spots on the next background row. When the pattern is being made, threads are picked up on both the pattern and background sheds.

When woven in plain weave, unequal horizontal bars are formed.

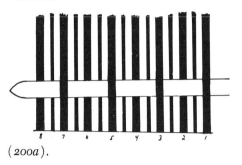

(200a).

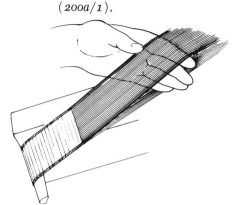

(200a/1).

For the traditional speckled background:

Raise the shed that has the background threads up. Beat. Weave all across.

Change sheds and beat. The pattern threads are now up.

Put your left hand into the shed, and hold the threads that are up.

With your right hand, start to insert the pick-up stick into the shed.

Transfer the border threads from your left hand onto the pick-up stick.

** Then, put the first, third, fifth and all the odd number pattern threads onto the pick-up stick. Drop the even threads.

This action will be like weaving in and out of the pattern threads on the top layer.

Transfer the left border threads onto the pick-up stick.

Turn the pick-up stick on edge to create a new shed.

Weave all across. Remove the pick-up stick.

Repeat all the above steps as written—except for the row marked **. For that row, put the second, fourth, sixth and all the even-numbered threads on the pick-up stick, and drop all the odd ones.

These directions are repeated over and over again to form

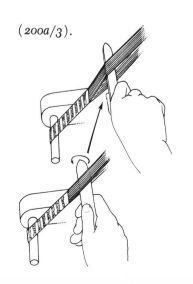

(200a/2).

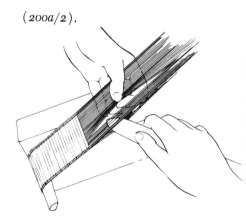

(200a/3).

the speckled background.

After a little practice, your eye will tell you whether you need to pick up an even or odd pattern thread.

Briefly, the steps for a speckled background are:

Raise the background threads. Beat.

Weave all across.

Change sheds, and beat—pattern threads are now up.

Pick up all the odd-numbered pattern threads.

Turn pick-up stick on edge and weave across row.

Change sheds and beat.

The background threads are up. Just weave across.

Change sheds and beat.

(*200a/4*).

Pick up all the even-numbered pattern threads.

Turn pick-up stick on edge and weave across.

Briefer yet:

Raise background threads and weave all across.

Raise pattern threads. Pick up all the odd-numbered pattern threads, and weave across.

Raise background threads and weave across.

Raise pattern threads. Pick up all the even-numbered pattern threads and weave across:

To Weave a Pattern with a Speckled Background:

Weave the speckled background until the pattern is to begin. Then:

PATTERN PICK-UP:

(*200a/5*).

Open the shed with the background threads up.

Hold the top layer in your left hand.

Into this shed, insert the pick-up stick from right to left.

Transfer the threads from the top layer onto the pick-up stick until you reach the area where the design is to begin.

In the area where you want a design, put every other thread on top of the pick-up stick. Make these first pick-ups match the speckled pick-ups from the previous row.

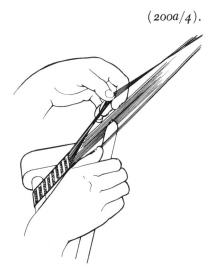

128

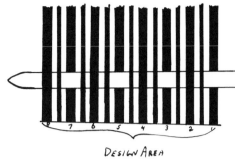

DESIGN AREA

(200b).

Turn the pick-up stick on end and weave across the row. Change sheds and beat.

The pattern threads are now raised and you will be weaving the speckled background.

BACKGROUND PICK-UP:

Hold the top layer in your left hand.

Insert the pick-up stick into this shed from right to left.

Put alternate pattern threads—AS WELL AS the design threads picked up in the previous row—on top of the pick-up stick. In the design area, all the pattern threads will be on top of the pick-up stick.

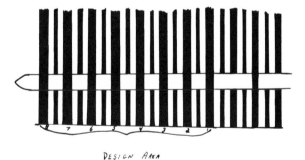

DESIGN AREA

(200c).

Turn the pick-up stick on edge and weave across the row.

Change sheds and beat. Background threads are now up.

PATTERN PICK-UP:

Hold the top layer in your left hand.

129

Insert the pick-up stick into this shed from right to left.
In the design area, put every other thread on top of the
pick-up stick.
These threads should be the *alternates* of the ones
picked up before.

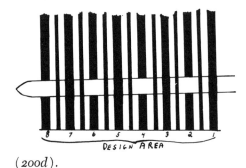

(*200d*).

Turn the pick-up stick on edge and weave across this
row.
Change sheds and beat. *Pattern threads* are now up.

BACKGROUND PICK-UP:

Hold the top layer in your left hand.
Put alternate pattern threads on top of the pick-up stick.
These are opposite to the ones picked up in the previous background row. Also, put all the pattern threads
that were picked up in the previous row on top of
the pick-up stick. In the design areas, all the pattern
threads will be on top of the pick-up stick.

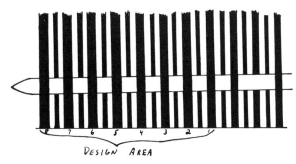

(*200e*).

Turn the stick on edge and weave across this row.

130

Briefly:

Pattern Pick-up—
> Background threads up.
>
> Pick up every other thread in the design area only.

Background Pick-up—
> Pattern threads up.
>
> Pick up alternate threads, and all pattern threads in the design area.

Pattern Pick-up—
> Background threads up.
>
> Pick up every other thread in the design area only. These should be alternates of the previous pattern pick-up.

Background Pick-up—
> Pattern threads up.
>
> Pick up alternate threads (opposite to those picked up in the previous background pick-up) and *all* pattern threads in the design area.

This is a bit tricky at first, but becomes routine after it's done for a while. I suggest that your first pattern be a simple geometric one. After you master this, just look at some of the great designs you can create.

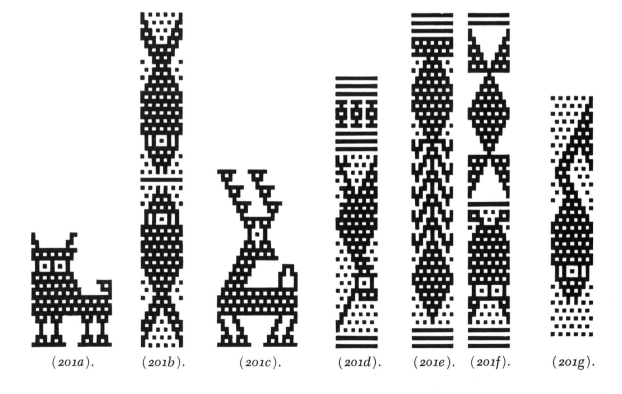

(201a).   (201b).   (201c).   (201d).   (201e).   (201f).   (201g).

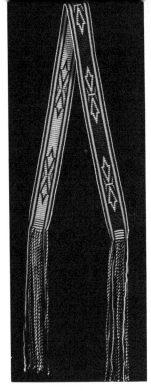

(202). Modern Navajo belt. Blue and white. *Courtesy— Muriel D. Fine, "Indian Country", Washington, D.C.*

(203). Close-up of the front and underside of a pattern in photograph (202).

(204). Another modern Navajo belt. Gold and white. *Courtesy—Muriel D. Fine, "Indian Country," Washington, D.C.*

(205). Close-up and underside of one pattern in photograph (204).

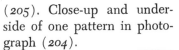

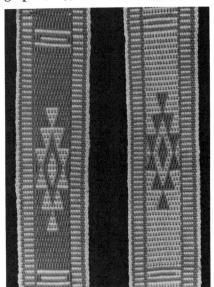

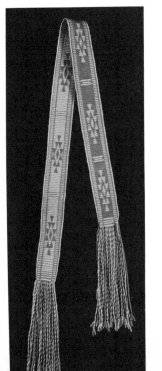

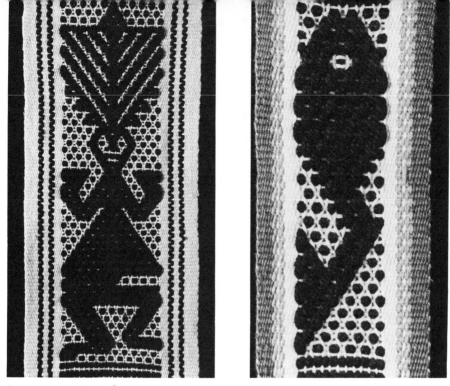

(206–217). Close-ups of patterns from Mexican belts.

(207).

(208).

(210).

(209).

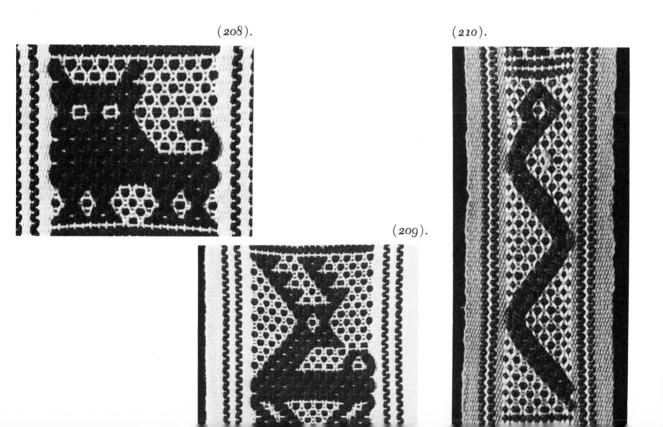

(211).

(212).

(213)

(214).

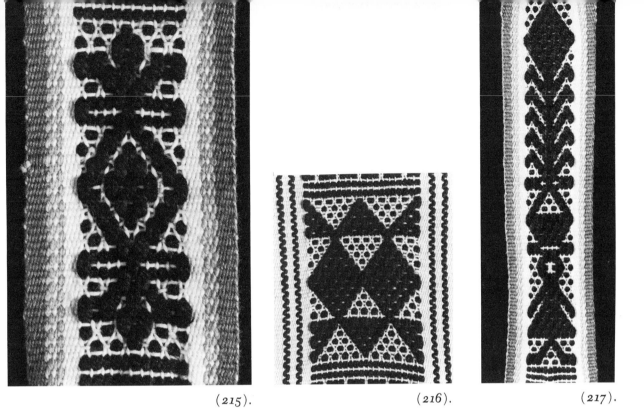

(215).   (216).   (217).

There are many, many ways to vary the pick-up techniques and patterns. When designing your warp, for example, part can be set up in a regular plain weave design, and part can be set up for a pick-up technique. The plain weave pattern can be large borders, or be placed within the body of the piece. You might make it symmetrical or asymmetrical.

Within the pattern area, you can have color changes. The color can change from thread to thread in rainbow order, perhaps, or the colors may be grouped in areas. The colors you choose may be bright, penetrating, peasanty, or bold. They could also be very subtle and sophisticated.

Perhaps you'd like to weave a large part of your piece in plain weave—and have just small areas of pick-up patterns. The reverse proportions could be attractive, too.

Ghiordes knots, loops, or wrapping can add solid color areas to an otherwise busy piece. Tie-dyed and space-dyed yarns can be used effectively with pick-up.

135

VII. *Finishing Off the Top—Topping Off the Bottom*

All good things must come to an end—and so it is with inkle bands. We must finish off the top—and top off the bottom. With a little thought and imagination, many interesting things can be done. How nice if these finishes can be imaginative and add a little extra sparkle or interest as well.

The finishing touches you choose can help coordinate your whole piece. Of course, they should suit the character of your piece and above all, they should be practical. A belt, for example, is designed to hold pants up: choose a good-looking but sturdy buckle, and sew it on *firmly*. If additional yarns or decorative items are used, the design, color, and texture of these items should blend well with the body of the piece.

Topping Off the Bottom

When cut from the loom, inkle bands usually have thick and colorful fringes. If you begin and end your band as suggested in the section on weaving, your ends are secure and your band won't ravel.

1. FOR A PLAIN FRINGE, you just need to trim your warp ends evenly.

2. NO FRINGE—ends sewn down.

(*218*). Extra long, dramatic fringe at end of the computer pattern belt, photograph (*38*). The numbers of threads used in each group varies. Colors are mixed sparingly. See color plate 2.

136

If no fringe is desired,

> Clip the end close to the last row of weaving.
> Fold the end under.
> Stitch it down as invisibly as possible.

3. TWIST

This method is so easy and so much fun to do that you'll find yourself unconsciously twisting every and all warp ends that come your way!

The number of warp ends you'll twist together will vary from piece to piece. For practice:

> With your right hand, pick up the first 3 warp ends.
> Hold them at the bottom, between your thumb and index fingers.
> Twist them to the right many times, until the strands feel rather stiff. (It's sometimes helpful to moisten your fingers a bit.)
> Pick up the next three warp ends and twist as before.
> Twist both groups together towards the left. (If you accidentally let go of the two groups at this time, they should twist together all by themselves. Magic? Well, the natural inclination of each group is to untwist itself. If you let go of them, they would start untwisting. Because the two groups are so close to each other, they just wrap around each other instead. Usually, they don't wrap around each other as neatly as they would if you guide them, however.)
> Secure them at the bottom with an overhand knot.

Twisting and the overhand knot shortens the final length of the fringe. The amount of the take up is about ½″ in every 6 inches.

(219). Finer threads were used in this band. Each twisted group has about the same number of threads in it. Care was taken to separate the colors as much as possible.

(220). This is the end of the Navajo belt that is shown in photograph (202). The twisted sections are even and neat, and little attempt has been made to separate colors.

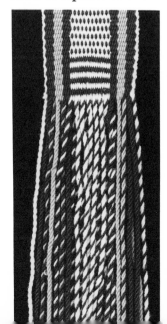

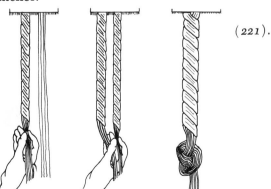

(221).

137

As you play with this twisting technique, you'll find several ways to achieve different effects.

1. All groups can be the same size.
2. Groups can vary in size.
3. Solid colors can be twisted together.
4. One color in one group and a different color in the other gives a "barber pole" effect.
5. Two or more colors in one group and two or more colors in the other, give a very busy look. I find this effect least pleasing of all for inkle bands.

4. WRAPPING

Wrapping can be done within a piece as well as on the fringes. Since the wrapping yarn can be of any color, it can help coordinate the piece. It is wrapped tightly around several warp threads, and helps to make a controlled, neat ending. Diagrams for this technique are on page 62.

5. BRAIDING

At one time or another, most of us have made a 3 strand braid. "Pigtails" work well on warp ends, too. I think the most effective braids are solid colored ones. Colors should be combined with discretion.

For practice, let's make a braid using 9 strands of yarn.

Divide the yarn into 3 groups.

Put the group on the right (A) over the center group (B).

Put the group on the left (C) over the new center group (A).

Right over the middle,

Left over the middle, and on and on.

An overhand knot at the end will keep it from coming undone.

(222/1). (222/2). (222/3). (222/4). (222/5).

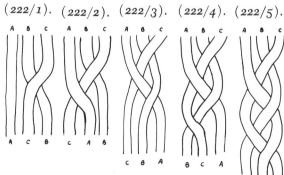

The braids can be the same size all across, or some can be fat and some skinny. My favorite combination is braids and twisted fringes.

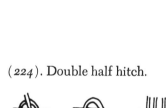

(*223*). Braids at the end of an inkle band. These will come undone if they are not tied or secured with an overhand knot. They also need to be trimmed.

6. TABS

Tabs can be effectively used at either the top or bottom of pieces such as wall hangings, pillows, purses, and necklaces. This weaving technique is fully described on page 69. Examples of this can be found in illustrations 92 and 94.

7. BEADS AND OVERHAND KNOTS

At the end of a sash, wall hanging, or a necklace, you might like to add some beads.

You can just thread your beads onto the fringe and hold them in place with overhand knots. You can space these beads randomly, or line them up very precisely.

8. MACRAMÉ

A touch of macramé can add a touch of elegance to an inkle band. The two knots most used in macramé are the square knot and the double half hitch. Step by step directions for making the square knot are shown in illustration 84. Here is the double half hitch.

(*224*). Double half hitch.

The variations possible with these two simple knots are endless. Let's discuss one simple way to end a piece with square knots. Please refer to the bibliography for further information on macramé.

Sennits or rows of square knots were used to end the sash in illustration 225. Here's how to do this:

Decide how long the row of square knots will be.

Cut a piece of yarn nine (9) times the length of the row.

Place the center of the yarn under a group of warp ends. (I used 10 warp ends for the sash pictured.)

Make a series of square knots, one below the other until the desired length is reached.

Either drop the ends of the knotting yarn and include them in the fringe, or

Hide the ends within the square knotted part. Thread the ends onto a tapestry needle and bring them into the center of the knotted row.

Repeat the preceding steps for each row of square knots you do.

The colors may be the same or different all across the row.

(225). Square knot sennits and twisting were combined to complete this hanging.

(226). Alternating square knot sennits finish off a little hanging.

(227). A grapevine branch was secured to the bottom of this hanging with double half hitches. Short sennits of square knots and half square knots were made below this. To finish it all off, another row of double half hitches was made, following the curve of the branch.

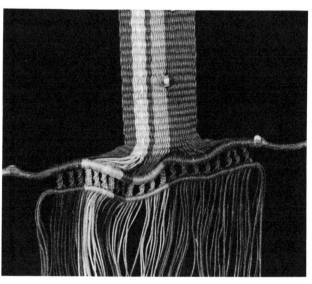

See also illustration 72.

9. TASSEL

How about a tassel at the end of a shade pull? Or, perhaps at each point of a pillow?

A piece of cardboard acts as a good gauge for your tassel. Cut the cardboard a little longer than you want the finished tassel to be. Use yarn that matches your inkle bands.

> Wrap your yarn around and around the cardboard until you think your tassel is "plump" enough.
>
> Cut two strands of yarn (approximately 12″ long).
>
> Slip these two strands of yarn under the yarn on the cardboard gauge.

(228). Fanciest shade-pull in town!

(229c).   (229d).

(229a).   (229b).

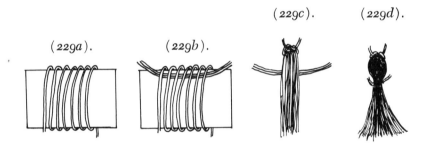

> Bring these strands to the top of the gauge, and tie them together VERY tightly.
>
> Cut the yarn at the bottom of the gauge and remove the gauge.
>
> Cut one or two more strands of yarn.
>
> Place the strands of yarn around the tassel about ¼ of the way down from the top.
>
> Tie these strands together VERY tightly.
>
> Trim the ends and attach the tassel to your inkle band.

10. BUCKLES

Buckles come in all shapes, materials, sizes, and colors. Choose a buckle and design a belt for it—or weave a belt—and choose an appropriate buckle for it!

141

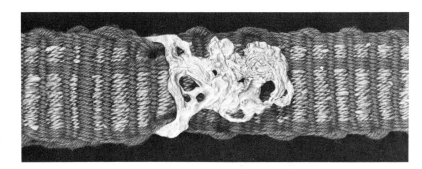

(230). Brass buckle on a belt in muted shades of rust.

(231). Big, showy, cast pewter buckle on a bright and bulky belt in blue and greens.

(232). Less showy, yet quite contemporary cast pewter buckle shown on an orange, gold, and brown belt.

Of course, a buckle must be sewn on securely. Cut your warp ends close to the end of the belt. Slip this end around the shank of the buckle, and sew it down firmly on the underside of the belt.

The other end of the belt can be finished as simply or as imaginatively as you please.

(233). LEFT: Two dainty buckles, patiently waiting for two dainty inkle belts.

(234). RIGHT: Don't the lines in this buckle strongly suggest a pick-up pattern? I think an interesting design could be adapted from it.

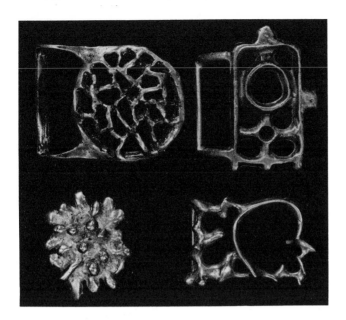

(235). Buckles—when viewed from this angle, and tops for wall hangings when turned around.

11. RINGS

Brass, bone, plastic, bamboo, copper, pewter—rings come in all kinds of materials. A very practical yet good-looking way to end an inkle belt is with two rings. These belts are adjustable and since rings have no prongs, there is little wear and tear on the fabric.

Metal rings can often be bought in hardware stores. Fabric shops carry some rings among their buckle displays. Some earring rings can be recycled—and you can even make your own rings.

Here are two different ways to use rings:

1. Attach both rings to one end of the belt.

    Cut the warp ends close to the end of the belt.

    Slip this end through both rings.

    Sew the end down securely on the underside of the belt. Leave a large enough hem so that the rings have a little room to move about. The other end of this belt can be finished very simply—or elaborately.

To fasten this belt:

Bring the end without the rings under the two rings

143

and push it through the center of the rings.
Bring it over the top ring and under the bottom ring.
Adjust it to your waist.
No need to worry—it stays in place securely!

(236).

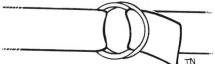

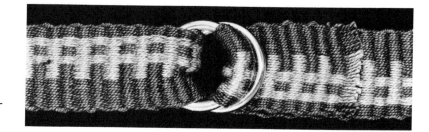

(237). Two brass rings complete this belt.

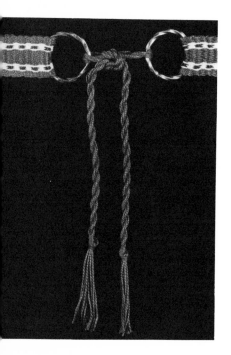

(238). One ring at either end of a belt, with a "tie" at the front.

2. Another way of using rings is this:
Make your belt a few inches smaller than your waist.
Clip the warp threads short on both ends of the belt.
Slip one end of the belt through one ring.
Sew this end down securely on the under side of the belt.
Repeat the last two steps for the other side of the belt.
With ribbon, leather thong, yarn—or whatever—make a "tie" about 2 feet long.
Put one end of the tie through one ring, the other end through the second ring.
Adjust this tie to your waist and secure it with a bow.

Finishing Off the Top

Wall hangings come in all shapes, sizes, colors, and degrees of sophistication. Some are just for fun—and may be light and

144

gay. Others may be somber, pretty, handsome, sophisticated, strong or delicate. All need to be hung in some way. The mood of the piece will influence your choice of finishing methods and materials.

So that the hanging doesn't collapse when hung, a stiff heading is almost always needed. This may be hidden in a hem, or become an obvious design element of the hanging.

Here are some accessories I always have on hand—and I'm always on the lookout for other possible candidates:

Wooden dowels
Plastic rods
Bamboo
Twigs and branches
Driftwood
Brass, copper and
    stainless steel rods
Wooden bars—both
    smooth and rough

Leather
Wooden knitting needles
Wooden embroidery hoops
Metal rings
Bamboo rings (usually sold
    as handles for handbags)
Wire
Exotic woods

(239). A common dowel has been carved out at either end. A twisted heading settles snugly into the grooves. The colors of the Ghiordes knots and the hanger are coordinated.

(240). Hiding behind this flap is a small stick with picture wire strung across it. A few square knots, and a curved row of double half hitches (see page 139) complete this flap.

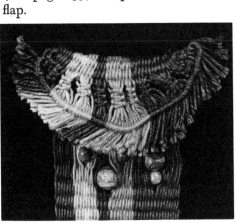

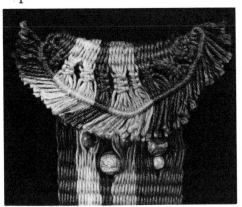

Many of these accessories can be woven directly into the

145

(241).

This Christmas bell pull is topped with two rings. The inner ring is a plastic bracelet wrapped with yarn; the outer ring a split bamboo ring painted red.

top and/or bottom of the hanging. If you want to weave in a stiff bar:

> Weave across with the regular weft thread.
>
> Into this same shed, insert the bar.
>
> Change sheds—and continue weaving with the regular weft thread.

Be sure to have several rows of weaving before and after the bar, so that the bar stays in securely.

If you choose to add the bar after the hanging is removed from the loom, weave a few extra inches for a heading. This may be turned under and hemmed, or brought forward to form a tab on top.

When you hem your piece, turn under enough fabric so that you can form a pocket big enough for the stiff bar to slip through. Hem this so that no stitches show through on the right side.

Perhaps you forgot to allow for a hem. If so, you might try this: Stitch, glue, or staple your hanging onto a scrap piece of wood. Glue (or use whatever method is appropriate to your materials) a decorative piece on top of this.

(242a). (242b).

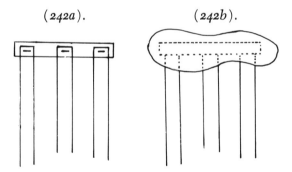

You now have a stiff framework for your hanging—but still no way to hang it.

If you like an invisible hanger, you can:

> 1. Sew a small ring(s) onto the back of the hanging, or
> 2. Stretch a strong string or wire tautly across the back. Attach the ends to the bar.

146

It's almost as much fun designing hangers that show, as designing the original inkle piece! Here are a few ideas:

1. Tie one or more leather thongs to either side of your bar. (See color plate 7D.)
2. Tie a few strands of yarn to either side of your bar. The predominant color of your band would probably be most effective.
3. Braid a few strands of yarn together for a hanger. Solid colors usually look most handsome in a braid.
4. A macramé hanger can be particularly nice. If you're not familiar with the technique, you may need some help from the books listed in the bibliography. (See photograph 95.)

   To a small ring, attach 6 strands of yarn. (The two outside strands should be four times as long as the finished strip. The four inner strands need only be a bit longer than the finished strip.)

   Using the two longer, outside cords as knotting cords, make a few square knots. (See page 63 for directions.)

   Slip a bead onto the center core cords.

   Continue making square knots below the bead. Add another bead or two if desired.

   Attach six more strands onto the ring. Make a second strip the same as the first.

   Knot the strips onto your bar.

   Make a few square knots below the bar.

   Trim the ends a few inches below the last square knot.

Innumerable variations are possible on this theme.

5. Twisted Hanger (see illustration 239).

   Take a few strands of yarn three times as long as your finished hanger will be. (The finished hanger will be *about* as thick as these strands.)

   At one end, tie all the strands together.

   Loop this end over some firmly fixed object, or have someone hold them for you.

   Hold the other end of the strands and move away

from the fixed ends until the strands are taut.

Twist them together clockwise until they are so taut that the yarn seems to be twisting back on itself.

Transfer the end to your left hand and grasp the center with your right hand.

Remove the other end from its moorings, and place it in your left hand also.

Let go of the center—and just watch as the two strands twist around each other counterclockwise.

Make an overhand knot a few inches from each end.

Attach to your bar.

Trim the ends.

Joining Forces

$$1—2'' \times 60'' \text{ inkle band} \div 2$$
$$\text{plus } 1—3'' \times 60'' \text{ inkle band} \div 2$$
$$\text{plus } 1—1\tfrac{1}{2}'' \times 60'' \text{ inkle band} \div 2$$
$$\overline{\text{equals } 1—13'' \times 13'' \text{ pillow}}$$

(243). Three, 60″ inkle bands—1—13″ × 13″ pillow.

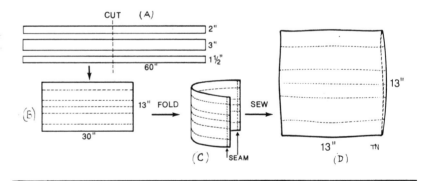

(244). Strips from three bands, arranged to form an interesting pattern for a pillow.

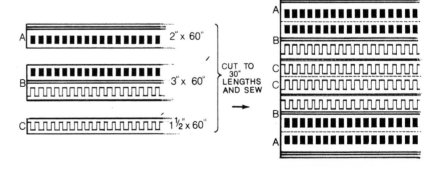

(245). And here's a finished pillow!

Yes, when inkle bands join forces, many interesting ideas evolve. By sewing strips together, you can make place mats, runners, purses, ponchos, vests, knapsacks, unusual wall hangings or, perhaps, a rug. You can even make a bedspread or upholstery fabric—but there is such a thing as carrying a good thing too far!

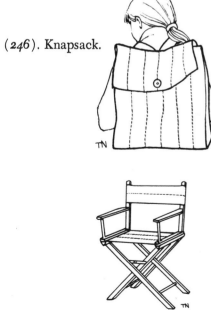

(246). Knapsack.

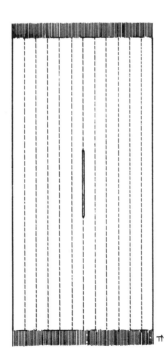

(248). Poncho.

(247). Director's chair.

To Join Strips Together by Hand

Personal preference and prejudice tell me that hand weaving deserves hand stitching, unless the machine stitching will not be visible.

MATERIALS NEEDED:

A blunt, large-eyed tapestry needle or bodkin. Yarn which is the same as the weft yarn used in the strips.

Thread the needle with one strand of the weft yarn.

Butt your strips together so that the patterns line up properly.

Start sewing or "weaving" your strips together three rows below the top.

Insert the needle through the end three warp threads on the strip on the right.

Put the needle through the end three warp threads on the strip on the left.

Pull the needle through and let a little "tail" of the thread extend out on the right.

Go to the second row from the top.

Insert the needle through the end three warp threads on the left strip.

Insert the needle through the first three warp threads on the right strip.

Draw the yarn through.

Go to the first row and proceed as before.

Now your thread is in securely, and you can proceed downward from top to bottom.

After you have finished the bottom row, end off by going over the previous two rows once more.

(249).

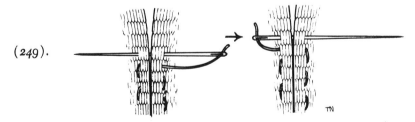

150

You have, in effect, woven the two strips together. The chances of them coming apart accidentally are practically nil. The join is so invisible that you'll have a very hard time telling where one strip ends and the other begins!

Sometimes, time is of the essence and you may feel the need for a quicker method of joining strips. If you have a sewing machine with a zigzag attachment, butt the two strips, and "zigzag" them together.

(250). Pattern for a vest.

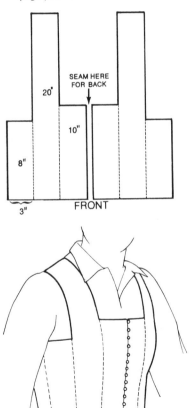

(251). Put a belt through the hem of this pouch or purse, and wear it around your waist.

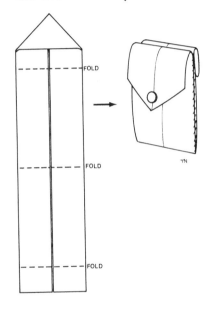

(252). Waist pouch or purse.

(253). Small poncho or Quechquemitl.

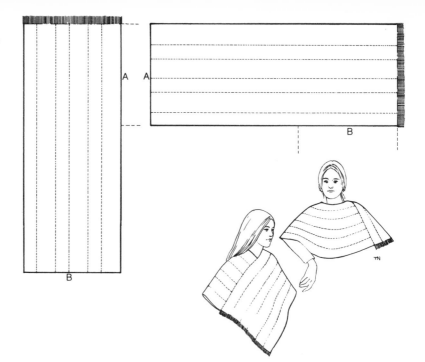

(254). Fold one strip up like this . . .

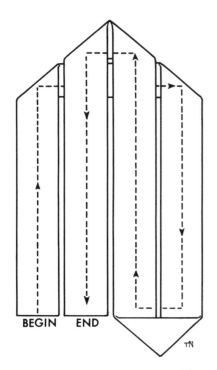

(255). . . . to get a wall hanging like this. *Yarns dyed by Martha Hoering (see color plate 7B.) Woven by Dan Bress. Designed by Helene Bress.*

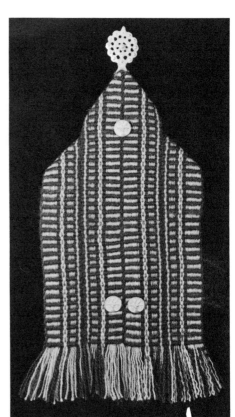

ARTICLE	FINISHED SIZE	NO. OF STRIPS NEEDED	SIZE EACH STRIP
1. Belt	Waist measurement plus a few inches for hems and overlap	1	any width x waist measure +
2. Bookmark	1″ x 9″	1	1″ x 9″
3. Choker	Neck measurement plus allowance for hems or tying.	1	any width x neck measure +
4. Eyeglass Case	3″ x 7″	1	3+″ x 19″
5. Guitar Strap	2–3″ x 60″	1	2–3″ x 60″
6. Knapsack	14″ high x 18″ wide x 5–7½″ deep Gusset for depth: 5″ or 7½″	2 ÷ 3 or 3 ÷ 2. 1 ÷ 2 { 1 ÷ 2 { 1 undivided	3″ x 105″ 3″ x 70″ 2½″ x 100″ 2½″ x 100″ 2½″ x 50″
7. Necktie	2–3″ x 58″	1	2–3″ x 60″
8. Pillow	13″ x 13″	3 ÷ 2	2″ x 60″
9. Floor Pillow	24″ x 24″	8 ÷ 2 or 4 ÷ 4	3″ x 52″ or 3″ x 104″
10. Pincushion	3″ x 4″	1	3+″ x 10″
11. Place Mat	12″ x 18″	1 ÷ 4	3″ x 80″
12. Poncho	36″ x 30″ (length as desired)	12	3″ x 66″
13. Purse— 　Evening 　Small Tote 　Large Tote 　Shoulder Strap	 4½″ x 7½″ (with flap) 10″ x 10″ 12″ x 12″ 2″ x 32″+	 1 ÷ 3 1 ÷ 3 or 1 ÷ 4 or 2 ÷ 2 2 ÷ 2 1	 2½″ x 40″ 3½″ x 80″ 2½″ x 104″ 2½″ x 52″ 3″ x 64″ from 2″ x 36″ to 2″ x 60″

ARTICLE	FINISHED SIZE	NO. OF STRIPS NEEDED	SIZE EACH STRIP
14. Quechquemetl	2 rectangles each 18″ x 43″	6 ÷ 2	3″ x 90″
15. Rug	3′ x 5′	12	3″ x 60″ plus fringe
16. Runner	15″ x 28″	2	3″ x 70″
17. Sash	Waist measurement plus about 40″ (20″ each side)	1	any width x waist measure plus 40″
18. Trims	Varies with article	varies	varies
19. Vest	Medium size—adjust width, length of strips for exact fit.	3 ÷ 4	a. 3″ x 56″ b. 3″ x 96″ c. 3″ x 48″

NOTE: BEFORE MEASURING A STRIP WHILE IT IS ON THE LOOM, release the tension completely.

(256). Rug.

Trims

You name it and you can probably make an appropriate inkle band to trim it with. Blouses, dresses, skirts, pants, ponchos, purses, pillows, curtains, window shades, lampshades, jewelry, boxes, candlestick holders, notebooks, placemats, blankets, bedspreads . . . and more.

Of course, you can sew the trims directly onto garments, but you can also fasten them on with snaps or pressure tape, such as "Velcro." This method allows you to interchange trims, and

154

to wash and clean the garment and trims separately.

Before you stitch your trims on permanently, take a few precautions. Clothing will either have to be washed or dry-cleaned. Be sure your trim is compatible with the fabric onto which it is sewn. It might be a good idea to wash the trim before it is applied to another fabric. If the trim will be exposed to direct sunlight, be sure that it is made of yarns that are fast to light. The labels on the yarns will often state this. Jute, for example, is notorious for fading in sunlight.

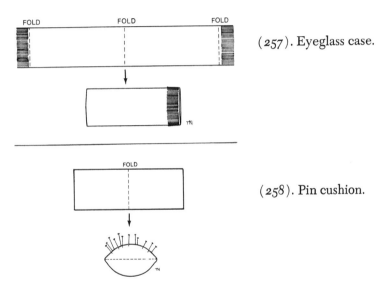

(257). Eyeglass case.

(258). Pin cushion.

(259). Bolivian purse made from strips.

155

(260).

(261).

(262).

(263).

156

(264).

(265).

(266). (267).

(269). LEFT: Napkin ring from Ecuador. *Gift from Allen Bress.*

(268).

(270). Swedish candlestick holder.

VIII. *Design It Yourself*

If you'd like a particularly satisfying experience, try designing your own pieces. I think you'll enjoy it.

Designing requires some concentration, thought, and decision making. This may be easy and natural for you—or it may be hard work. Sometimes ideas may flow freely—sometimes you may have to work hard to corral them. There is always a certain amount of agonizing, doubt, wonder, and suspense. "Will it turn out to be the thing of beauty I anticipated?" Maybe it will —maybe it won't completely measure up to your expectations. Well, there's always a next time, and almost always you'll have a special feeling when looking at a piece you designed yourself. "Look what I did!", you'll say to yourself, and perhaps you'll share your pride with a few choice friends.

Color

A yarn shop could be your initial source of inspiration. Have you ever walked into a well-supplied yarn shop and just stood there admiring the vast range of colors and types of yarns? Soon, you find you're drawn towards some yarns more than others. You pick up one skein, and look at it longingly. Then you wander around and choose another and think how well they'd go together. Keep going—and choose a third color and perhaps a buckle or some beads that go with the yarn. And there you'll have the beginning of an appealing band.

I'm a collector. When I see some yarn that appeals to me, I buy it, even though I may not have a particular project in mind for it. I do the same for beads, buckles, and other interesting accessories. I find that the yarns and accessories I choose usually are quite companionable. The eventual marriage of the two is generally a happy one.

Since individual taste is usually quite consistent, I believe that this system may work for you, too. You would tend to build up a supply of yarns and accessories that suit your needs and personality.

Nature is rich in fine color schemes. A spectacular sunset may challenge you to create a spectacular color scheme for your next project. Then there are autumn leaves, fire, landscapes and flowers.

Seashells or a collie dog may inspire rather quiet, subtle combinations, but a parrot, peacock, or tropical fish may inspire brilliant and imposing ones. Once you tune yourself to the fact that there is color all around you, you'll keep adding to the above brief list.

There are many beautiful nature books available and these, too, are fun to use for inspiration.

Paintings by the old masters or the moderns can be yet another source of color consideration. Then there are traditional fabrics from countries such as Mexico and Peru as well as traditional Oriental and Navajo rugs.

If you are to capture the feel of the color scheme from a painting or a peacock feather, for example, you'll need to observe the proportions of one color to another. Blue, green, and red in equal proportions will give quite a different feel from much blue, a little green and a hint of red.

Pattern

With just three colors and fifty threads, almost a trillion, trillion different inkle patterns can be created—and that's just in plain weave. I wonder what the figure would be if it included pick-up patterns?

Plain weave patterns are created from the basic design elements as shown on pages 36 to 39. How simply or fancifully you put the elements together will depend upon the effect you want. If you're designing a belt that will be worn with a flowered skirt, you'll want to keep the pattern on the belt quite simple and unobtrusive. Perhaps the belt would be almost a solid color, with just a little square in another shade or color. In this way, the skirt and the belt would complement each other. A belt that will be worn with a solid colored outfit could be as patterned as you please.

It's fun to take some crayons, pastels, water colors, or felt tipped pens and play with the design elements. You'll find that you can design some very respectable bands. After a while, you'll become so familiar with the design possibilities that you'll be able to create patterns as you warp the loom.

It isn't often that a painting, animal, or natural object will directly inspire a plain weave patterned inkle band, but occasionally it does happen. Just take a look at the lava lizard below.

(*271*). This lava lizard all but says, "I'll make a great plain weave inkle band. Draw me!" (*Photographed on the Galapagos Islands*).

 (*272a*). And so, I "drew" him.

(*272b*). Draft for (*272a*).
W = White; G = Gray; B = Black.

O	W W W W W G G G W W B B G G B G G B B W W G G G G W W W W W
H	W W B W W G G G B W W G G G W B W G G G W W B G G G W W B W W

Although inkle bands are narrow, they can be sewn together to make wider pieces such as pillows, purses, wall hangings, ponchos, and rugs. Since more than one band is usually used and since the joins can be made practically invisible (see illustration 249, page 150), the pattern can be designed in such a way that the finished piece appears as one wide pattern rather than several small ones. For example, does this look like six individual strips of inkle bands, or like one wide piece of cloth?

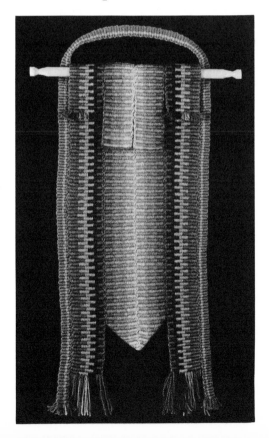

(*273*). Wall hanging. Three bands were woven, cut or shaped, and sewn together to make this hanging. See color plate 7A. *Designed by Helene Bress. Woven by Dan Bress.*

161

If the patterns on the individual strips are completely symmetrical, they will line up and look like this.

(274). Simple, symmetrical band.

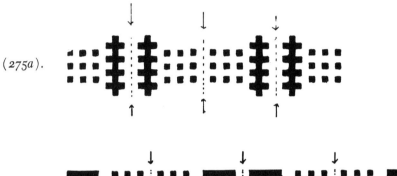

(275a).

(275b).

If the patterns are not completely symmetrical, joined patterns from the same band will widen visually.

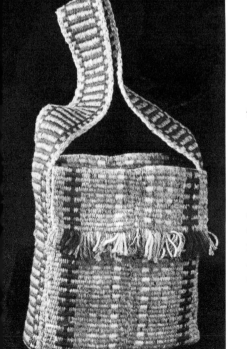

(276). Purse. One strip was cut in half, faced in opposite directions and sewn together for the body of this purse. Another strip forms the handle, and gusset or side panels.

162

The resulting patterns are of more interest than several symmetrical bands lined up.

A second and/or third patterned band can be added for yet more diversity. See illustrations 245 and 256 for some other examples of this.

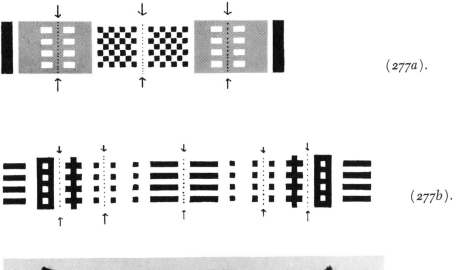

(277a).

(277b).

(277c). Just two differently patterned bands were woven for this runner.

When you're planning to join strips together, try to have the selvedges on all the strips the same color. It's best to use the same color and weight of weft thread for all the strips, too. The joinings will be least visible in this way.

Pick-Up Patterns

Pattern is everywhere—and almost any small pattern can be adapted to one or another of the pick-up techniques. It's quite helpful to fully understand the pick-up techniques, though, before trying to design for them. Each one has its own assets and limitations and it is important to keep these in mind. For example, one technique always has bars in the background and floats that are over three threads. In another, the floats can be of any length. However, the fabric won't be practical if the floats are much longer than three or four threads.

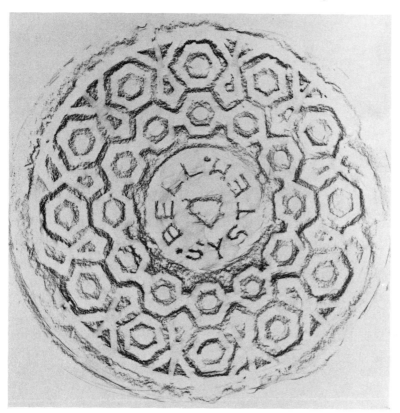

(278). On the campus of the University of Maryland are some delightful manhole covers. Here's a rubbing of one that lends itself well to pickup designs.

(279). Your own initials can be the starting point for a unique design. Here's how Doramay Keasbey used hers.

Traditional folk motifs are generally quite adaptable to the pick-up techniques. You probably have a storehouse of some of these in your mind—chevrons, eight-pointed stars, or perhaps some bird motifs.

There's a vast amount of these folk art motifs from every part of the world—Sweden, Finland, Denmark, Iceland, Rumania, Peru, Mexico, Russia, Lapland, Greece, Guatemala, New Zealand—to name a few. Then, there are the North American Indian traditional designs. Oriental rugs, cross stitch patterns, plain and fancy geometrical designs are still other sources.

Most often, the patterns you observe or design yourself will have to be modified somewhat to fit the requirements of the weave and the final use of your piece.

(280). The design for this choker was adapted from a Russian carpet. See text.

The pattern on the choker in illustration 280 was adapted from a small section of a Russian carpet. Although it still retains the "feel" of the original design, it has been modified considerably. The design was scaled down and simplified to suit the number of threads it could be conveniently woven on. The original was red and blue with touches of other colors scattered throughout; blue and green was chosen for the choker. I was careful that the floats never exceeded four threads.

The Greek fabric in illustration 281 has intrigued me for a long time. I have adapted a section of this for a pick-up weave, and plan to weave a belt with the adapted design.

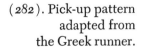

(282). Pick-up pattern adapted from the Greek runner.

(281). Wide, woven runner from Greece. The pattern is adaptable for inkle weaving. *Gift of Dr. and Mrs. Leonard Meinwald.*

Adding Width

Inkle weaving, by its nature, produces long, narrow strips. For many things, such as belts, sashes, and chokers, this is just fine. There are many times, however, when a wider looking piece is preferred.

We have discussed earlier that strips can be sewn together. You can design several strips in such a way that, when sewn together, the pattern appears as one wide pattern rather than several small ones.

Instead of sewing strips together, there are times when you might want to place strips side by side to make a wider piece. Flat and/or three dimensional hangings can be formed in this way (see color plate and illustration 150).

By weaving in weft materials that extend beyond the selvedges, a wider appearance will result, too. Bamboo, dowels, plastic strips, unspun wool, reeds, long strands of yarn, wire, feathers, dried flowers, twigs . . . are just a few things you might like to try. The method for weaving with these extra weft materials is discussed on page 59.

Also, two strips can be woven side by side on the inkle loom. Occasionally, they can be bound together with a rigid weft such as a dowel.

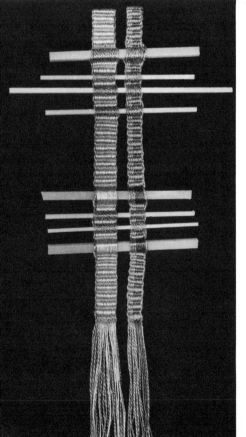

(283). Miniature hanging. Two narrow strips were woven side by side on the loom. Plastic bars were woven in occasionally.

How the beginning and ending of a hanging is handled is quite important. An otherwise narrow hanging will appear somewhat broader and substantial with a top piece that extends beyond either side of the fabric (see illustration 80). If the "hanger" of the piece extends below the dowel or top bar, that will help to widen the appearance, too.

At the bottom, a twig, dowel, or other appropriate material can be woven in, or sewn into, a hem.

Ideas from the Warp Itself

I always warp my inkle loom with the maximum length of yarn it will hold. Often, several projects can be made on just one warp. Even if I don't have many ideas to begin with, ideas usually flow as the weaving progresses. Seldom is there enough warp to try out all of these ideas.

(284). G = Gold; Y = Yellow; O = Orange.

O	G O O O O O O O O O O O O O O O O O G G G Y Y G G G O O O G G G Y Y G G G
H	G G G G G G G G G G G G G G G G G G G G Y Y G G G O O O G G G Y Y G G G

(continued:)

O O O O O O O O O O O O O O O G
G G G G G G G G G G G G G G G G

On a wide, orange and gold linen warp, I did a long hanging with deep orange beads and Ghiordes knots. Having accomplished what I set out to do, I now felt free to experiment with the remaining warp. Two hangings with areas of unwoven warp and one neckpiece were the results of this.

(285–288). Four different
pieces woven on the same
warp.

(285).

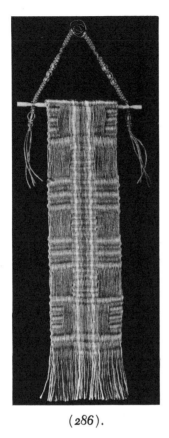

(286).

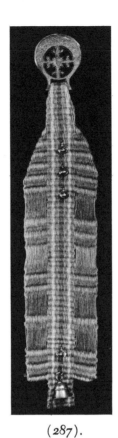

(287).

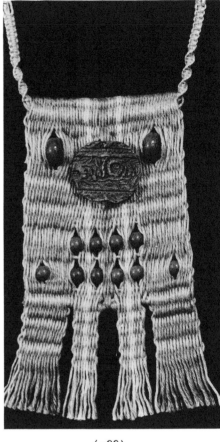

(288).

On another warp, I made a small hanging (illustration 118),
a double faced necklace with a slit down the center (illustration 88) and then removed many of the center and outer light-
colored threads to make a darker and narrower hat band (illustration 79).

On a narrow blue and green warp, earmarked for pick-up patterns, I made a

> Choker and necklace to match.
> Choker with bells on one end.
> Choker with macramé and beads.
> Trim for a dress, and a
> Book mark.

Different warps suggest different kinds of projects.

Off You Go

There is a vast range of colors, patterns and designs, techniques, and materials to choose among. You can get texture and dimension with Ghiordes knots, fringes, loops, and textured yarns. You can enhance your piece with beads, slits, picots, tabs, and macramé.

You can use linen, wool, cotton, and synthetics. The yarns can be heavy, textured, smooth and fine. All the colors of the rainbow are yours. Beautiful space-dyed yarns are available—or you can tie-dye your own. And there is a wide range of patterns and designs.

Inkle weaving a narrow field? Humbug! It's as wide as your imagination!

IX. *Mystery History*

Inkle, inkle, little band
How I wonder in what land
Someone first did you create
And your name originate.

> Your illusive history
> Seems to shroud in mystery
> Place and time and even spelling
> But this question's most compelling:

Why am I so fascinated
By your patterns complicated?
By what force are modern hands
Charmed with making ancient bands?

> Wound on pegs through loops of string,
> Threads become a useful thing,
> Either plain or fancy bordered
> Formed the way the threads are ordered.

Now I wonder, having started,
How from this can I be parted?
For I'd gladly weave away,
Inkle, inkle all the day.

DORAMAY KEASBEY

In 1545 "pieces of white unckle for girdles and lates (laces)" were purchased for 7d.[1]

In 1567, one penny was paid for "whyte incle to make synes in books."[1]

(*289*). Modern Swedish slot and heddle device. All the techniques described in this book can also be done on the slot and heddle frame. Warp threads go through a hole and a slot alternately. The threads in the holes remain stationary, while the threads in the slots move up and down to form the sheds. Many of the old slot and heddle frames are elaborately carved.

(*290*). Tape loom. For centuries, narrow tapes and bands were made on tape looms. Although utilitarian tapes were the usual order of the day—towel hangers, shoe ties and the like, inkle-type bands could be, and occasionally were, made on tape looms.

Shakespeare, Chaucer, and Swift refer to "inkles".

"Lord!" says Jonathan Swift in *Polite Conversations*, "why she and you were as great as two inkle weavers. I am sure I have seen her hug you as the devil hugg'd the witch."

What were they all talking about? What is an inkle? Most historic sources agree that it is some kind of narrow band or tape.

Tapes and bands can be woven on a tremendous variety of looms and in an equally tremendous variety of techniques.[2]

In this country, we have come to accept Mary M. Atwater's concept of inkle looms and inkle weaving. In the 1930's, Mrs. Atwater imported from England what was probably the first inkle loom to come to this country. The directions that came with it were for plain weave bands only. It was suggested that these might be enhanced with embroidery. "This seemed to me quite an uninteresting business," she said.[3] Well, she had a very inquisitive mind, and a broad knowledge of weaving techniques. Through experimentation she found that many of the beautiful and elaborate band weaves that were done in Europe and other parts of the world on the hole and slot or slot and heddle devices could be adapted for the inkle loom. She also found that Navajo, Guatemalan, Mexican, and other native American belt weaves worked well on the inkle loom, too.

It is from this base that our present ideas of inkle weaving have evolved. Mary Atwater did much creative thinking and appears to have led us in new and innovative directions.

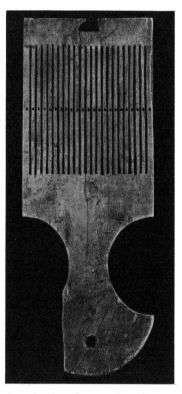

(*291*). Another style of tape loom. The weaver puts the curved part between his knees and supports the loom in this way. The bottom left section is broken off.

Appendix

Key — H = Heddle
      O = Open (the open spaces between the heddles)

Illustration 37a
Yarn — Rug yarns wool
Weft — doubled
Number of threads — 69
Width — 3″
Technique — plain weave
Draft:

O	W	W	W	W	W	W	B	B	B	W	W	W	W	W	W	W	W	W	W	W
H	W	W	W	W	W	W	B	B	B	W	W	W	G	G	G	G	G	G	G	W	W

(*continued*)

O	W	W	W	W	W	W	W	W	W	W	W	W	W	= 34
H	W	W	W	W	W	W	W	W	W	W	W	W	W	W	= 35

                                                          69

COLOR KEY — W = white (off-white); B = black (charcoal); G = gold (bright).

Illustration 37b
Yarn — Acrylic – mixed weights
Weft — 1 strand, 4 ply yarn (knitting worsted wt.)
Number of threads — 55
Width — 2⅜″
Technique — plain weave
Draft:

O	R	R	R	R	R	R	W	W	W	B	B	B	B	B	W	W	W	R	R	W	B	B	W	R	R	R	= 27
H	R	R	R	R	R	R	W	W	W	W	W	W	W	W	W	W	W	R	R	W	B	B	W	R	R	R	= 28

                                                                            55

COLOR KEY — R = red; W = white; B = blue.

Illustration 37c
Yarn — Perle cotton #3
Weft — single
Number of threads — 119
Width — 3¼″
Technique — plain weave
Draft:

```
O | O O O T T T T T T T T T G G G O O G G G T T T T T T T T T T T G G G G G G G G
H | O O O T T T T G G G G G G G G O O O G G G G G G G G T T T T G G G T T T T T
```

(*continued*)

```
O | T T T O O T T T G G G G G G G G O O O      = 59
H | T T T O O O T T T T T T T T G G G G O O O = 60
                                                  119
```

COLOR KEY — O = olive green (dark); T = turquoise (bright); G = green (light).

Illustration 37d
Strip from Bell Pull
Yarns — Acrylic – four ply – knitting worsted type – bulky
Weft — doubled
Number of threads — 45
Width — 2¾″ +
Technique — plain weave
Draft:

```
O | R R R W W W W W W W R R W W W W W W W W R R R      = 22
H | R R R W W W W R R R R R R R R R R W W W R R R = 23
                                                       45
```

COLOR KEY — R = red; W = white.

Illustration 37e
Yarn — Perle #5
Weft — single
Number of threads — 45
Width — ⅞ inches
Technique — plain weave

Draft:

```
O | Y Y Y Y Y Y  Y Y Y Y Y Y Y Y Y Y Y Y  Y Y Y Y Y   = 22
H | Y Y Y Y Y Y  G G G G G G G G G G  G Y Y Y Y Y Y   = 23
                                                        45
```

COLOR KEY — Y = yellow; G = green.

Illustration 37f
Yarn — Light weight crochet cotton
Weft — single
Number of threads — 55
Width — 1″
Technique — plain weave
Draft:

```
O | B B B B B B B B W W W W  B  B  B  W W W W  W B B B B B B B B   = 27
H | B B B B B B B B B  B  B  B  W W W W  B  B  B  B B B B B B B B B = 28
                                                                    55
```

COLOR KEY — B = blue (medium); W = white.

Illustration 37g
Yarn — Perle cotton #3
Weft — 4 strands
Number of threads — 69
Width — 1¾″ +
Technique — plain weave
Draft:

```
O | O O O O O O O O O O O O O O O O O O G G G T T T T G G G O O O O   = 34
H | O O O O O O O T T T T G G G G G G G G  G G G G G G G G O O O O O  = 35
                                                                      69
```

COLOR KEY — O = olive (dark); T = turquoise (bright); G = green (light).

Illustration 37h
Woven by James L. Kapplin
Yarn — Wool – fine, approx. 4500 yds. per pound
Weft — single
Number of threads — 95
Width — 1⅜″
Technique — plain weave

Draft:

```
O │ B B B B B B B B B B B B B B B B B B B B B B B B B B B B B B B B
H │ B B B B B P P P P P B B B B B P P P P P B B B B B P P P P P B B B B B P P P P
```

(*continued*)

```
O │ B B B B B B B B B B B   = 44
H │ B B B B P P P P B B B B  = 45
                            89
```

COLOR KEY — B = brown; P = pale blue.

Illustration 37i
Kite tail (woven by Dan Bress)
Yarn — Perle cotton #3
Weft — doubled
Number of threads — 47
Width — 1¼″
Technique — plain weave
Draft:

```
O │ R R R R W B B W R R R R R R R R W B B W R R R   = 23
H │ R R R R W W W W R R R R R R R R W W W W R R R R  = 24
                                                    47
```

COLOR KEY — R = red; W = white; B = blue.

Illustration 37j
Woven by Dan Bress
Yarn — Crochet cotton – regular weight
Weft — 2 strands
Number of threads — 59
Width — 1″
Technique — plain weave
Draft:

```
O │ T T T T T T T T T T T T T T T P P T T T T P P T T T T P P T   = 29
H │ T T T T T T T T T T T T T T T T P P T P P P P P P P P T P P T T  = 30
                                                                    59
```

COLOR KEY — T = turquoise; P = purple.

176

Illustration 37k
Yarn — Wool – fine, approx. 1800 yds. per pound
Weft — single
Number of threads — 117
Width — 2¾″
Technique — plain weave
Draft:

```
O│O O O O O O O P P P P P H G G G G O O O O H H H H b Y Y Y Y b  H H H H O O O
H│O O O O O O O T T T T T Y Y B B B B B O O O O  G G G b T T T b  G G G O O O
```

(*continued*)

```
O│O G G G G G H P P P P P O O O O O O O    = 58
H│O B B B B B Y Y T T T T T O O O O O O O = 59
                                             117
```

COLOR KEY — O = orange; P = purple; T = turquoise; Y = yellow; H = hot pink; G = green;
B = brown; b = black.

Illustration 37l
Strip from runner
Yarn — Acrylic – 4 ply, bulky knitting worsted type
Weft — doubled
Number of threads — 49
Width — 3¼″ – (a bit less)
Technique — plain weave
Draft:

```
O│R R R R R R R R R R R R W R R R R R R R R R = 24
H│R R W W W W R R W W W W R R W W W W W W W W R R = 25
                                                   49
```

COLOR KEY — R = red; W = white.

Illustration 37m
Yarn — Tapestry wool – 4 ply
Weft — doubled
Number of threads — 42
Width — 1¾″
Technique — plain weave

Draft:

```
O│D D D D M M M L L L L L M M M D D D D    = 20
 ├──────────────────────────────────────────────
H│D D D D M M M L L M D M L L M M M D D D D = 21
 └──────────────────────────────────────────────
                                      41
```

COLOR KEY — D = darkest green; M = medium green; L = light green.

Illustration 37n
Yarns — Nylon and perle cotton
Weft — double strand
Number of threads — 113
Width — 2½″
Technique — plain weave
Draft:

```
O│C C C C B B B B B B B B B C C B B B B B B B R N N N N N N N N R B B B B B C
 ├──────────────────────────────────────────────────────────────────────────
H│C C C C B B B B B B B B B C C B B B B B B B R N N N L L L N N N R B B B B B B
```

(*continued*)

```
O│C B B B B B B B B B B B C C C C    = 56
 ├──────────────────────────────────────
H│C C B B B B B B B B B B B C C C C = 57
 └──────────────────────────────────────
                                 113
```

COLOR KEY — C = chartreuse; B = blue (royal); R = red; N = navy blue; L = light blue.

Illustration 37o
Woven by James L. Kapplin
Yarns — Cotton: Rust and black = #5 perle; blue = floss
Weft — doubled
Number of threads — 48
Width — ¾″ +
Technique — plain weave
Draft:

```
O│R R R B B B B B R R R R R R R B B B B B B R R R = 24
 ├──────────────────────────────────────────────────
H│R R R L L L L L R R R R R R R L L L L L R R R = 24
 └──────────────────────────────────────────────────
                                              48
```

COLOR KEY — R = rust; B = black; L = light blue.

Illustration 37p
Yarns — Red = floss; Green = perle #5; Black = perle #3
Weft — single
Number of threads — 61
Width — 1⅜″
Technique — plain weave
Draft:

```
O | R R R R R R R R G G G G B B B B G G G G R R R R R R R R     = 30
  |------------------------------------------------------------
H | R R R R R R R R G G G G G B B B G G G G G R R R R R R R R R = 31
                                                              61
```

COLOR KEY — R = red; B = black; G = green.

Illustration 37q
Yarn — Rust = floss; Gold and Orange = jute and rayon mixture
Weft — 4 strands
Number of threads — 89
Width — 1¾″ —
Technique — plain weave
Draft:

```
O | R R R G G G G G G G G G G R R R R R O O O O O O O O O O O O O O O
  |-----------------------------------------------------------------
H | R R R G G G G G R R R R R R R R R R R R R R R R R R R R R R R R R
```

(*continued*)

```
O | O O O O O O O R R R   = 44
  |-------------------------
H | O O O O O O O O R R R = 45
                        89
```

COLOR KEY — R = rust; G = gold; O = orange.

Illustration 37r
Yarn — Light weight rug yarn
Weft — doubled
Number of threads — 59
Width — 2¼″
Technique — plain weave

Draft:

O	A A A A A A A A A A A A A A C C A A A A A A A A B B A A	= 29
H	A B B B B B B B B B B B A A C D C A A E E E A A B B A A	= 30

59

COLOR KEY — A = deep purple; B = hot pink; C = light lavender; D = dark lavender; E = blue-purple.

Illustration 37s
Yarn — Perle cotton #5
Weft — single
Number of threads — 71
Width — 1⅜″
Technique — plain weave
Draft:

O	B B B R W W W W W W W W B B R W W W W W R B B W W W W W W W W
H	B B B R W W W B B B B B B B B R W W W W R B B B B B B B B B

(*continued*)

O	W W R B B B	= 35
H	W W W R B B B	= 36

71

COLOR KEY — B = blue; W = white; R = red.

Illustration 37t
Designed and woven by Dan Bress
Yarn — Black = perle #5; Royal blue = perle #3; Yellow = perle #3
Weft — doubled
Number of threads — 56
Width — 1⅜″
Technique — plain weave
Draft:

O	B B B B B B B B B R R R R R R R R R B B B B B B B B B B	= 28
H	B B B B B B B B B R R R R Y Y Y Y R R R R B B B B B B B B	= 28

56

COLOR KEY — B = black; R = royal blue; Y = yellow gold.

180

Illustration 37u
Yarn — Crochet cotton – heavy weight
Weft — one strand
Number of threads — 49
Width — 1¼″ +
Technique — plain weave – Because of the double warp threads in one spot, the brown weft peeps through a little. Also, the double yellow is slightly raised.
Draft:

O	B B B B Y Y Y Y D D Y Y Y Y B B B B B B B B B B	= 24
H	B B B B B B B B Y Y Y B B B B B B B B B B B B B	= 25
		49

COLOR KEY — B = brown; Y = yellow; D = double yellow.

Illustration 37v
Yarn — Floss
Weft — 1 strand
Number of threads — 53
Width — 1″
Technique — plain weave
Draft:

O	B B W W W W W W B B B W W B B B B R R B B B B B B	= 26
H	B B W W W R W W W B B B W W B B B B R R B B B B B B	= 27
		53

COLOR KEY — B = blue (medium); W = white; R = red.

Illustration 37w
Yarns — Acrylic – 4 ply – knitting worsted type (black and bright rust);
Acrylic – 2 ply – novelty yarn (gray-white flecked, textured slightly)
Weft — doubled
Number of threads — 49
Width — 2⅜″
Technique — plain weave
Draft:

O	B B G G G G G G G G G G G G G G G G B B B B B	= 24
H	B B B B B G G R R R R G G G G G B B B B B B B B	= 25
		49

COLOR KEY — B = black; G = gray; R = rust.

Illustration 37x
Yarns — Acrylic – 4 ply
Weft — tripled
Number of threads — 67
Width — 2½″ +
Technique — plain weave
Draft:

O	O O O O O O O O O B B B G G R R R G G G B B B O O O O O O O O	= 33
H	O O O O O O O O O B B B O O O R R R O O O B B B O O O O O O O O	= 34

67

COLOR KEY — O = orange (reddish); B = brown (dark); G = gold; R = rust (deep).

Illustration 38
Yarn — Rug yarn – Acrylic – machine washable and dryable
Weft — doubled
Number of threads — 45
Width — completed – 2½″
Technique — plain weave (beaten rather hard – rather stiff)
Draft — slightly adapted at the edges so that the weft won't show.

O	C B B B B B B B B B B B B B B B B B B B B B C	= 22
H	C C C C B C B B C B C C C C B C B B C B C C C	= 23

45

COLOR KEY — C = chartreuse; B = blue (bright).

Illustration 40
Yarns — Rug wool – and Nubby wool – (2 ply – but coarse)
Weft — single
Number of threads — 27
Width — 2⅜″
Technique — plain weave
Draft:

O	R R R N N N N N N N R R R	= 13
H	R R R N N R R R R N N R R R	= 14

27

COLOR KEY — R = rust (vegetable dyed with coreopsis); N = natural (wound with rust and y
low. Occasional nubs).

Illustration 41
Yarn — Linen – 10/3 – orange; orange – nubby cotton and linen novelty yarn
Weft — 4 strands
Number of threads — 37
Width — ⅞″
Technique — plain weave
Draft:

O	O O N N N N N N N N N N N N O O	= 18
H	O O N N N O O O O O O O N N N O O	= 19

37

COLOR KEY — O = orange; N = nubby – orange and yellow.

Illustration 42
Yarn — Singles wool – spun lightly – about size of 4 ply knitting worsted
Weft — doubled
Number of threads — 35
Width — 2⅞″
Technique — plain weave (with *much* trouble)
Draft:

O	B B B B B B B B B B B B B B B B B	= 17
H	B B B B B R R R R R R R B B B B B	= 18

35

COLOR KEY — B = brown, dark; R = rust.

Illustration 43
Yarn — Handspun, vegetable dyed wool – color changes are almost invisible except for the yellow
Weft — 1 strand
Number of threads — 35
Width — 2″
Technique — plain weave
Draft:

O	B B B B B B B B B B B B B B B B B	= 17
H	B B G G G B R R R R R B Y Y Y B B B	= 18

35

COLOR KEY — B = brown (medium); G = gold; R = rust; Y = yellow.

Illustration 47
Yarns — Perle cotton #3; floss
Weft — 1 strand
Number of threads — 17
Width — ¼" +   Picot extends beyond this
Technique — plain weave, picot, button woven in
Draft:

O	G G G G G G G	= 8
H	G G G B B B B B G	= 9

17

COLOR KEY — G = green (kelly); B = blue (bright).

Illustration 48
(*Drafts for 48, 49, 50b, 63, and 69 — are all the same. Other information differs.*)
Yarn — Floss – 6 strand
Wefts — 1. Floss – one strand for plain weave throughout
              2. Perle cotton – #3 – white – 1 strand for picots
Number of threads — 53
Width — 1" + picot length
Technique — plain weave with picots
Draft:

O	B B W W W W W W B B B W W B B B B R R B B B B B B	= 26
H	B B W W W R W W W B B B W W B B B B R R B B B B B B	= 27

53

COLOR KEY — B = blue; W = white; R = red.

Illustration 49
Yarn — Floss – 6 strand
Wefts — 1. one strand – for plain weave
              2. picot and fringe weft = doubled floss – various colors
Number of threads — 53
Width — 1"
Technique — plain weave, picots on one side, long fringe on other (for knotting, etc.)
Draft — *same as 48*

Illustration 50b
Yarn — Floss – 6 strand – background: medium blue, white and red
Wefts — 1. floss – 1 strand – for plain weave throughout

184

2. perle cotton #3 – white for picots
Number of threads — 53
Width — 1″ + picot length
Technique — plain weave with picots on either side
Draft — *same as 48*

Illustration 63
Yarn — Floss – 6 strand
Wefts — 1. 1 strand floss
       2. 3 strands floss for picots
Number of threads — 53
Width — 1″
Technique — plain weave with uncut fringe
Draft — *same as 48*

Illustration 69
Yarn — Floss – 6 strand
Wefts — 1 single used throughout for plain weave
4 strands floss, together, for fringe
Number of threads — 53
Width — 1″ + fringe – (2½″ wide at widest point)
Technique — plain weave – with fringes
Draft — *same as 48*

Illustration 72
Yarns — Fine background thread – cotton 24/3
Heavy pattern – floss
Weft — fine thread – doubled
Number of threads — background: 36
               pattern: 15
             total: 51

Width — ⅝″
Technique — basketweave background pick-up
Draft:

O	F F F H F F H F F H F F H F F H F F H F F H F F F	= 25
H	F F H F F H F F H F F H F F H F F H F F H F F H F F	= 26

                                           51

COLOR KEY — F = fine – medium green; H = heavy pattern – bright blue.

Illustration 73

Yarn — Perle cotton, and floss
Weft — single strand #5 perle plus plastic bars
Number of threads — total = 47 (left section = 30, right section = 17)
Width — small section = ½″ +, large section = ¾″, widest point = 7½″
Length — 12″
Technique — weft brought up at end of one group; second shuttle from there to end
Draft:

O	G G G G G G G G G G G G G G G
H	G T T T T T T T T T T T T T T T

Left Section

O	G G G G G G G G
H	G G G B B B B B G

Right Section

COLOR KEY — G = green (kelly); T = turquoise; B = blue (bright).

Illustration 74

Yarn — Mixture of acrylics and wool novelty yarns
Weft — doubled – fingering weight yarn
Number of threads — 65
Width of woven band — 2″
Width of hanging at widest point — 9¼″
Length of hanging — 17″
Technique — plain weave with bars and dowels woven in –
differing widths change the pattern in the band
Draft:

O	W W B B B B B B W W G G G W W R R W W G G G W W B B
H	W W W W W W W W W W W W W W W W W W W W W W W W W W W

(continued)

O	B B B B W W	= 32
H	W W W W W W W	= 33

65

COLOR KEY — W = white with flecks of red and yellow; B = blue (royal with loops);
R = red – unevenly spun; G = green – kelly – with some blue flecks.

Illustration 77
Yarns — Mixture of acrylics and wool novelty yarns
Weft — doubled – fingering weight yarn
Number of threads — 65
Width of band — 2″
Width of tree at widest point — 10¼″
Height of tree — 11½″
Technique — plain weave with plastic bars and dowels woven in
Draft — *same as 74*

Illustration 78
Yarn — 6 strand floss
Weft — floss doubled – used on each row
Plastic bars and thin rods – woven in on black shed. Discarded earring woven in at top
Number of threads — 87
Width — band 2″ + tree at widest point — 10″
Technique — plain weave
Draft:

```
O | B B B B B B B B B B B B B B B B B B B Y Y B Y Y B B B B B B B B B B B B B
H | B B B R R R R R R R R R R R R R B B Y Y B B Y Y B B R R R R R R R R R
```

(*continued*)

```
O | B B B B B B   = 43
H | R R R R B B B = 44
            87
```

COLOR KEY — B = black; R = red (bright); Y = yellow-gold.

Illustration 79
Yarn — Cottolin – combination of linen and cotton
Weft — doubled
Number of threads — 25 (from original of 107 threads)
Width — ½″
Technique — plain weave with feathers woven in
Draft:

```
O | B B G G R T R R G G B B   = 12
H | B B G G R R R R R G G B B = 13
              25
```

Warp — Threads were removed from the cottolin hanging and necklace in *photograph 118.*
Edge gold and black threads were cut out; all center gold ones were removed.

COLOR KEY — B = brown; R = rust; T = *two* rust threads together – side by side; G = gold.

Illustration 80
Hanging
Yarn — 10/5 linen
Weft — 1 strand
Number of threads — 83
Width — 3″; Height — 22″
Technique — plain weave, with beads woven in. The macramé at bottom was done off loom.
Draft: *same as photograph 99*

Illustration 81
Yarns — Acrylics – royal blue – 4 ply knitting worsted type;
kelly green – 2 ply – about same weight as the blue
Weft — 2 shuttles – fine = 1 strand; heavy = 6 strands;
also rods and bells. Shuttles alternated.
Number of threads — 56
Width — 2¾″; height — 31″
Technique — plain weave, weaving in bars, adding bells at edges, wrapping.
Draft:

O	B B B B B B B B B B B B B B B B B B B B B B B B B B B B	= 28
H	B B B B G G G G G G G G G G G G B B B G G G G B B B	= 28

56

COLOR KEY — B = blue (royal); G = green (kelly) with flecks.

Illustration 85
Yarn — 10/5 linen
Weft — 1 strand
Number of threads — 83
Width — 3″
Height — 23½″
Technique — plain weave, slits woven in, beads woven in, tabs at bottom, macramé at top.
Draft — *same as photograph 99*

Illustrations 87, 88, and 89
Yarns — Cottolin – a combination of linen and cotton
Wefts — doubled
Number of threads — 107
Width — completed — 2¼″
Technique — plain weave with beads and bells woven in
Draft — *same as 118*

Illustration 94
Yarn — 10/5 linen
Weft — single
Number of threads — 107
Width — 4″
Height — 8¾″
Technique — plain weave; beads woven in – warp and weft;
tabs at end – tie woven in and then knotted.
Draft:

O	G O O O O O O O O O O O O O O O G G G Y ·Y G G G O O O G G G Y Y G G G
H	G G G G G G G G G G G G G G G G G G G G G Y Y G G G O O O G G G Y Y G G G

(*continued*)

O	O O O O O O O O O O O O O O O O G = 53
H	G G G G G G G G G G G G G G G G G = 54

107

COLOR KEY — G = gold; Y = yellow; O = orange.

Illustration 95
Yarn — 10/5 linen
Weft — 1 strand
Number of threads — 107
Width — 4⅛″
Height — 16½″
Technique — plain weave and warp unwoven in areas; heading – macramé
Draft — *same as 94*

Illustration 96
Yarn — 10/5 linen
Weft — single

Number of threads — 107
Width — 4″
Height — from top of heading — 21″
Techniques — plain weave; bells woven in; warp unwoven in areas
Draft — *same as 94*

Illustration 99
Hanging
Yarn — Linen 10/5
Weft — 1 strand; pottery beads
Number of threads — 83
Width — 3″
Height — 27″
Technique — plain weave; beads woven in; tube; bar woven in
Draft:

O	O O O O O O G G G G G G O O O T T T T T T T T O O O O O O O O
H	O O O O O O O G G G Y Y G G G O O O T T T T T T T T O O O O O O O O

(*continued*)

O	O O O O O O O	= 41
H	O O O O O O O O	= 42

83

COLOR KEY — O = olive green; G = gold; Y = yellow; T = orange.

Illustration 101
Yarns — Warp-linen – 10/5
Weft — 1 strand; Ghiordes knots, wool and acrylics, 4 ply, several strands together
Number of threads — 107
Width — 3⅛″ (where Ghiordes knots flair out – width increases to almost 6″);
8¾″ = bar at top
Height — 36″ +
Technique — plain weave and Ghiordes knots, beads woven in, twisted hanger.
Draft — *same as 94*

Illustration 105
Yarn — 6 strand floss
Weft — doubled

Number of threads — 87
Width — completed — 2″ +
Technique — plain weave
Draft:

O	B B B B B B B B B B B B B B B B B B Y Y B Y Y B B B B B B B B B B B B B
H	B B B R R R R R R R R R R R R R B B Y Y B B Y Y B B R R R R R R R R R R

(*continued*)

O	B B B B B B B	= 43
H	R R R R R B B B	= 44

87

COLOR KEY — B = black; R = red (bright); Y = yellow-gold.

Illustration 106
All same information as 105,
EXCEPT:
Weft — Black floss doubled — and used on each row; Plastic bars woven on *red* shed.

Illustration 107
All same information as 105,
EXCEPT:
Weft — Black floss doubled — and used on each row; Plastic bars and thin rods woven in on *black* shed.

Illustration 108
Yarns — Acrylics — 4 ply knitting worsted type;
2 ply — bulky novelty — about same weight as the 4 ply
Wefts — 2 shuttles: fine = 1 strand; heavy = 6 strands
Number of threads — 56
Width — 3″ +
Technique — plain weave — 2 shuttles alternating throughout — heavy and fine
Draft — *same as 81*

Illustration 115
Yarn — gold Lamé
Weft — 1 strand
Number of threads — 31

Width — ¾″ minus
Technique — plain weave — with beads woven in
Draft:

```
O │G G G G G G G G G G G G G G     = 15
H │G G G G G G G G G G G G G G G   = 16
  └─────────────────────────────
                               31
```

COLOR KEY — G = gold (lamé)
Beads — mottled gold and orange; mottled brown.

Illustration 116
Yarns — Linen — 10/5
Weft — single; beads
Number of threads — 31
Width — 1¼″
Technique — plain weave with beads woven in
Draft:

```
O │G G G G G G G G G G G G G G     = 15
H │G G G G G G G G G G G G G G G   = 16
  └─────────────────────────────
                               31
```

COLOR KEY — G = gold.

Illustration 117
Same draft and weaving information as in 72

Illustration 118
Yarns — Cottolin — a combination of linen and cotton
Weft — doubled
Number of threads — 107
Width — completed — 2¼″
Technique — plain weave — with beads and a bell woven in
Draft:

```
O │G G G B G G M M G G R R R G G G G G G G G G G G G G G G G G G G G G G G
H │G G G B G G M M G G R R R G G G G G G G G G G G G G G G G G G G G G G G
  └──────────────────────────────────────────────────────────────────────
```

(*continued*)

| O | G G R R R G G M M G G B G G | = 53 |
| H | G G G R R R G G M M G G B G G G | = 54 |

107

COLOR KEY — G = gold; B = black; M = brown; R = rust.

Illustration 121
Yarn — Acrylic — 4 ply — knitting worsted type — solid color and spaced dyed yarns
Weft — single
Number of threads — 75 (37 – pattern, space dyed; 38 – solid blue)
Width — 3¼″
Technique — pick-up — horizontal stripe technique — pattern based on a Peruvian design
Draft:

| O | B B S S B S S S S S S S S S S S S S S S S S S S S S S S S S S S B S S B B | = 37 |
| H | B B B B B B B B B B B B B B B B B B B B B B B B B B B B B B B B B B B B B B | = 38 |

75

COLOR KEY — B = blue (solid, royal); S = space dyed — white *to* pale green *to* olive green.

Illustration 123
Yarn — Acrylic — space dyed and solid — 4 ply knitting worsted type
Weft — doubled
Number of threads — 67
Width — completed — 2¾″
Technique — plain weave — using space-dyed yarns randomly
Draft:

| O | R R R R R R R R B B B S S S D D D S S S B B B R R R R R R R R | = 33 |
| H | R R S S S S S S S S B B B S S S D D S S S B B B S S S S S S S S R R | = 34 |

67

COLOR KEY — R = rust; S = space-dyed — yellow, gold; browns,
B = brown; D = dark rust.

Illustration 124
Yarn — 4 ply knitting worsted, wool, space-dyed very subtly;
4 ply knitting worsted, wool, solid
Weft — single
Number of threads — 33
Width — 1⅞″
Technique — plain weave; warp-space dyed, adjusted deliberately
Draft:

```
O | G G G G G G G G G G G G G G G      = 16
H | G G S S S S S S S S S S S G G = 17
                                        33
```

COLOR KEY — G = green (olive); S = space-dyed.
Space dyed yarns adjusted in the warping so that they line up
approximately at the same point throughout. — Very subtle changes. — Looks tie-dyed.

Illustration 125
Yarn — Acrylic — 4 ply — knitting worsted type; solid color and space-dyed
Weft — doubled
Number of threads — 41
Width — 1⅞″
Technique — plain weave with areas of space dyed yarns, adjusted deliberately
Draft:

```
O | T T T T T T T T T T T T T T T T T T T T      = 20
H | T T T T S S S T T S S S T T S S S T T T T = 21
                                                  41
```

COLOR KEY — T = turquoise (medium); S = space-dyed (light blue, bright turquoise, green).

Illustration 126
Yarn — Acrylic — 3 ply — light weight — usually used for baby sweaters and accessories.
Very stretchy
Weft — doubled
Number of threads — 33
Width — 1⅛″
Technique — plain weave. Made an attempt to line up spots
— as in space dyed yarns. Too stretchy. — Didn't work

194

Draft:

O	W W W W W W W W W W W W W W W W	= 16
H	W W W W W W W W W W W W W W W W W	= 17

33

COLOR KEY — W = white, with occasional dashes of blue, green, and yellow.

Illustration 127
Yarns — Knitting worsted — wool — 4 ply; loop mohair, space-dyed, wool
Weft — quadrupled
Number of threads — 37
Width — 1⅝″
Technique — plain weave
Draft:

O	P P P S S S S P B B P S S S S P P P	= 18
H	P P P P P P P P P B B P P P P P P P P P	= 19

37

COLOR KEY — P = purple; S = space-dyed (reds, oranges, and golds); B = black.

Illustration 129
Hanging — tie-dyed warp
Yarns — Rug *wool*
Weft — single
Number of threads — each strip 53
Width — each strip — 3″; hanging — 12″ wide × 19″ high
Technique — plain weave with a tie-dyed warp
Draft:

O	T T T T T T T T T T T T T T T T T T T T T T T T T T	= 26
H	O O O O O O O O O O O O O O O O O O O O O O O O O O O	= 27

53

COLOR KEY — O = olive (solid); T = tie-dyed.

Illustration 138
Yarns — Background — 3 strand cotton — approximately same as #5 perle;
Pattern — floss — doubled
Wefts — 1. 1 strand for plain weave throughout; 2. 2 strands floss for pattern.
Number of threads — 123
Width — 2¼″
Technique — Brocade (pick-up)
Draft:

O	Brown 61 ×
H	Brown 62 ×

COLOR KEY — B = brown.

Illustration 151
Yarns — Background: fine — cottolin. Pattern: heavy — 2 ply novelty knitting yarn, acrylic
Weft — single, fine background thread
Number of threads — 57 (Background – 40; Pattern – 17)
Width — 1″ to 1¼″ — strips vary
Technique — basketweave background pick-up
Draft:

O	F F F Y F F Y F F Y F F O F F O F F Y F F Y F F Y F F F	= 28
H	F F Y F F Y F F Y F F Y F F O F F Y F F Y F F Y F F Y F F	= 29
		57

COLOR KEY — F = fine background, brown cottolin;
Y = heavy pattern — yellow novelty yarn; O = heavy pattern — orange.

Illustration 152
Same information as 72

Illustration 155
Yarns — Fine background — cottolin (3200 yards per pound); Heavy pattern —
Rya rug yarn (570 yards per pound)
Weft — cottolin — single strand
Number of threads — strips 1, 2, 4, 5: 81 (background — 56, pattern — 25);
strip 3: 75 (background — 56, pattern — 19)
Width — 1½″ to 2″
Technique — basketweave background pick-up
Size of hanging — 12″ wide by 17″ long

Draft — strips 1, 2, 4, 5:

O	F F F B F F B F F G F F G F F G F F G F F G F F G F F G F F G
H	F F B F F B F F B F F G F F G F F G F F G F F G F F G F F G F

(*continued*)

O	F F B F F B F F F	= 40
H	F B F F B F F B F F	= 41

81

Draft — strip #3: On either side of strip #3, three brown pattern threads have been removed while on the loom

COLOR KEY — B = heavy pattern — brown; G = heavy pattern — gold; F = fine.

Illustration 156
Yarns — Perle cotton #5 — background; Perle cotton #3 — doubled-pattern —
Weft —
Number of threads — 62 (Background — 43, Pattern — 15, Border — 4)
Width — 1⅜″
Technique — basketweave background pick-up
Draft:

O	F F H F F F H F F H F F H F F H F F H F F H F F H F F F H F F	= 31
H	F F H F F H F F H F F H F F H F F H F F H F F H F F H F F H F F	= 32

63

COLOR KEY — F = fine background thread (white); H = heavy pattern thread (two shades of red).

Illustrations 157, 158, 159, 160, 161, 162, 163, 164, 165, and 166
Information same as in 156

Illustration 167
Yarns — Background — rayon — 800 yards/lb. Pattern — rayon — 800 yds./lb.,
doubled. Border — rayon — 800 yds./lb.— single strand.
Weft — doubled
Number of threads — 81 (Pick-up pattern threads – doubled – 11;

two border threads on either side — doubled — 4; remaining threads — single — 66)
Width — 3½″
Technique — plain weave border pattern, combined with basketweave background pick-up
Draft:

```
O | D B B B T T F H F F H F F H F F H F F H F F H F F T T T T T T T T B B B B

H | D B B B B T T F F H F F H F F H F F H F F H F F F F F F F F F F T T T B B B
```

(*continued*)

```
O | B B D   = 40

H | B B B D = 41
              81
```

COLOR KEY — F = fine white background; D = 2 "F" threads together;
H = pattern doubled; B = blue rayon; T = turquoise.

Illustrations 168, 169, 170
Same information as in 167
EXCEPT:
Weft — single

Illustration 171
Same information as 150

Illustration 172
Yarns — Perle cotton #5: Background — single;
Pattern — doubled
Weft — Perle #5, single
Number of threads — 61 (doubled threads — 10; all others — 51)
Width — 1¾″
Technique — plain weave borders, with basketweave background pick-up
Draft:

```
O | B B B B B D B R R B T B B T B B T B B T B R R B B B B B B B B   = 30

H | B B B B D B B D R R B B T B B T B B T B B R R B B B B B B B B B = 31
                                                                      61
```

COLOR KEY — B = black — single; R = red — single; D = 2 strands of red together;
T = 2 white strands together.

Illustration 173
Same information as 172

Illustration 174
Same information as in 172
EXCEPT:
Number of threads — 61 (doubled threads: 18; others: 43)
Draft:

O	B B B B B D B D D B T B B T B B T B B T B D D B B B B B B	= 30
H	B B B B D B B D D D B B T B B T B B T B B D D B B B B B B B B	= 31

61

COLOR KEY — B = black — single; R = red — single; D = red — doubled;
T = white — doubled.

Illustrations 175, 176
Same information as in 172

Illustrations 177 — 179
Same information as in 72

Illustration 180
Yarn — Background: perle cotton #3 — single; Pattern: perle cotton #3 — doubled.
Weft — doubled
Number of threads — 67 (Pattern — 17; others — 50)
Width — 2″
Technique — basketweave background pick-up
Draft:

O	Y Y D Y Y Y B Y Y B Y Y B Y Y B Y Y B Y Y B Y Y B Y Y B Y Y D Y Y	= 33
H	Y Y D Y Y B Y Y B Y Y B Y Y B Y Y B Y Y B Y Y B Y Y B Y D Y Y	= 34

67

COLOR KEY — Y = yellow — single; D = dark brown — single;
B = brown — doubled pattern thread.

Illustration 183a
Yarns — Background — 10/2 cotton; pattern — floss
Weft — single

Number of threads — 47 (Pattern — 19; Background — 28)
Width — ⅞″
Technique — horizontal stripe background pick-up
Draft:

O	F F H H H H H H H H H H H H H H H H H H H F F	= 23
H	F F F F F F F F F F F F F F F F F F F F F F F F	= 24

47

COLOR KEY — F = fine (10/2 cotton black) = background; H = heavy
(floss dark red) = pattern.

Illustration 186
Yarn — Heavy weight crochet cotton
Weft — single — blue (not the same color as the edge threads
and therefore forms a little pattern at the edge.)
Number of threads — 73 (Pattern — 25; Other — 48)
Width — 1⅜″
Technique — horizontal stripe pick-up
Draft:

O	B B B B B P P P P P P P P P P P P P P P P P P P P P P P P P B B B B B B	= 36
H	B B G G B B B B B B B B B B B B B B B B B B B B B B B B B B B B B B G G B B	= 37

73

COLOR KEY — B = black; G = green; P = pattern thread (pale blue).

Illustration 187
Same information as in 186

Illustration 188
Yarn — Perle cotton #3
Weft — doubled
Number of threads — 55
Width — 1¾″ — minus
Technique — horizontal stripe pick-up
Draft — *same as 189*

Illustration 189
Yarn — Perle cotton #3
Weft — single
Number of threads — 55

Width — 1¾″ +
Technique — plain weave
Draft:

O	B B B B B B B B B B B B B B B B B B B B B B B B B B B	= 27
H	B B G G G G G B B O O O O O O O O O O O O O O B B	= 28

55

COLOR KEY — B = brown; G = gold; O = orange.

Illustration 190
Yarn — Acrylic — 2 ply, and 2 strands bulky acrylic yarn
Weft — 4 strands
Number of threads — 55
Width — 2¼″
Technique — plain weave
Draft:

O	B B G G G G G G G W H B B B H W G G G G G G G B B	= 27
H	B B B B B B B B B B B B B B B B B B B B B B B B B B B B	= 28

55

COLOR KEY — B = brown (medium, soft brown); G = gold (soft);
W = white (off-white); H = bulky white (extra heavy)

Illustration 191
Yarn — Acrylic — 2 ply — and two strands of heavy, *bulky* 4 ply
Weft — single
Number of threads — 55
Width — 2⅜″
Technique — plain weave with horizontal stripe pick-up
sometimes on light layer, sometimes on dark
Draft — *same as 190*

Illustration 193
Same information as in 121

Illustration 195
Yarns — Background: cotton about 8/4 (carpet warp) — 800 yards per pound;
Pattern — cotton — 3 to 4 times heavier than the background thread.
Weft — cotton — about 8/4 — red

Number of threads — 68 (Pick up pattern — 11; Border and background — 57)
Width — 2⅛″
Technique — speckled background pick-up
Draft:

```
O | R R R R R B Y B R R B B B B B B B B B B R R R B Y B R R R R R R R = 34
H | R R R R R B Y B R R Y Y Y Y Y Y Y Y Y Y R R B Y B R R R R R R R = 34
                                                                      68
```

COLOR KEY — Y = yellow — finer weight; R = red — finer weight;
B = black — 3 to 4 times heavier than above.

Illustration 196
Yarns — Background: cotton — about 8/4 carpet warp — 800 yds./lb.;
Pattern: cotton — same size as above — but tripled
Weft — single — red
Number of threads — 60 (Pattern pick-up — 11; All others — 49)
Width — 1⅝″
Technique — speckled background pick-up
Draft:

```
O | R R R R B Y B R R Y Y Y Y Y Y Y Y Y Y Y R R B Y B R R R R R = 30
H | R R R R B Y B Y R R H H H H H H H H H H R B Y B R R R R R = 30
                                                              60
```

COLOR KEY — R = red — single strand; Y = yellow — single strand;
B = black — doubled; H = heavy pattern thread (black tripled)

NOTE: This is the draft exactly as it was threaded on this belt.
However, the eighth thread in the "Heddle" row was probably meant to be Red.

Illustration 197
Yarns — Background: cotton — about the weight of carpet warp — 8/4 (800 yds./lb.);
Pattern: cotton — 3 to 4 times heavier than the background thread
Weft — cotton — about 8/4 used singly — white
Number of threads — 71 (Pattern pick up — 11; All others — 60)
Width — 2¼″
Technique — speckled background pick-up
Draft:

```
O | G G G G G G P P W W W W B B B B B B B B B B B W W W W P P G G G G
H | G G G G G G P W P W W W W W W W W W W W W W W W W W W P W P G G G
```

(continued)

O	G G	= 35
H	G G G	= 36

71

COLOR KEY — G = green (lt. wt. cotton); P = pink (lt. wt cotton);
W = white (lt. wt. cotton); B = black (heavy wt. cotton).

Illustration 198

Yarns — Background — cotton — about 8/4 carpet warp size (800 yds./lb.);
Pattern and border accent threads — cotton — 3 to 4 times heavier than background thread.
In pattern area this is doubled.
Weft — cotton — finer weight, used singly.
Number of threads — 113 (Pattern pick-up — 21; All others — 92)
Width — 3¾″
Technique — speckled background pick-up
Draft:

O	F F F F F F F H F F F H F F F F F F F F F F F F F F F F F F F F F F F F F F
H	F F F F F F F H F F F F H F F F F H H H H H H H H H H H H H H H H H H H H

(continued)

O	F F F F H F F F H F F F F F F F F	= 56
H	F F F F H F F F F H F F F F F F F F	= 57

113

COLOR KEY — F = fine (yellow); H = heavy (black).

Illustration 202

Warp — Wool — 4 ply knitting worsted respun very tightly
Weft — single cotton — 8/4
Number of threads —
      Pick up pattern threads = 20
      All others   = 69
             Total   89
Width — 2⅝″
Technique — speckled background pick-up
Draft:

203

Illustration 210
Same information as in 195

<pre>
                        20
                    ⁀⁀⁀⁀⁀
O │W B B B B G G G B B B W   B B B G G G B B B B W   = 44
H │W B B B B G G G B B B B   B B B B G G G B B B B W = 45
                    ⁀⁀⁀⁀⁀   89
                        20
</pre>

Colors — B = blue; G = grey; W = white.

Illustration 204
Warp — Wool — knitting worsted — respun very tightly
Weft — 8/4
Number of threads —
Pick-up pattern threads = 24
All other threads   = 69
                           ――
                           93
Width — 2⅝″
Technique — speckled background pick-up
Draft:

<pre>
                        24
                    ⁀⁀⁀⁀⁀
O │W G G W W W W W W G G W   G G G G G G G G G W   = 46
H │W W G G G G G G G G G   G G W W W W W W G G W W = 47
                    ⁀⁀⁀⁀⁀   93
                        24
</pre>

Colors — G = gold; W = white.

Illustration 206
Same information as in 198

Illustration 207
Same information as in 197

Illustrations 208, 209
Same information as in 198

Illustrations 211, 212
Same information as in 197

Illustration 213
Same information as in 198

Illustration 214
Same information as in 196

Illustration 215
Same information as in 197

Illustration 216
Same information as in 198

Illustration 217
Same information as in 197

Illustration 230
Yarn — Acrylics — 4 ply knitting worsted type;
Other is 3, 2 plied yarns — (maroon, rust, brown) — wound onto a spool side by side, but not plied together.
Weft — 1 strand — 4 ply yarn
Number of threads — 51
Width — 2⅜″
Technique — plain weave
Draft:

O	R R D R R D D D R R R R R D R R D D D D R R R R	= 25
H	R R D R M M M M M M M M M M D R R M M M M R R R R	= 26

51

COLOR KEY — M = multi-colored; R = rust; D = dark rust.

Illustration 231
Yarns — Acrylics — 4 ply knitting worsted type;
2 ply — bulky novelty yarn, about the same weight — but a little
bulkier appearing than the 4 ply knitting worsted.
Weft — fine = 1 strand; heavy = 6 strands — 2 shuttles
Number of threads — 56

Width — 3″ +
Technique — plain weave — with 1 shot heavy weft, 1 shot fine weft.
The second half of the belt is woven — Heavy, fine (6 times),
fine, heavy, fine, fine. Repeat.
Draft — *same as 81*

Illustration 232
Yarn — Acrylic
Weft — tripled
Number of threads — 67
Width — 2½″ +
Technique — plain weave
Draft:

O	O O O O O O O O B B B G G R R R G G G B B B O O O O O O O O	= 33
H	O O O O O O O O B B B O O O R R R O O O B B B O O O O O O O O	= 34

67

COLOR KEY — O = orange (reddish); B = brown (dark); G = gold; R = rust (deep).

Illustration 237 is the same as 37g

Illustration 238 is the same as 37i

Illustration 241 is the same as 37d
EXCEPT:
Technique — plain weave — bells woven in.
Rings added on top — spiral sennits around inner one.

Illustration 245
Pillow — 3 different strips combined
Yarns — Acrylics — Background: flecked yarn — 4 ply knitting worsted type;
Others — solid colors

STRIPS #I AND #VI
Weft — doubled; Number of threads — 57; Width — 2½″; Technique — plain weave
Draft:

O	O O O B B B B B B B O O O O O O O O O O O O O O O O O O O	= 28
H	O O O B B O O O B B O O O O O O G G G O O P P P P O O O	= 29

57

COLOR KEY — O = orange flecks; B = brown; G = gold; P = pale orange.

STRIPS #II AND #V
Weft — doubled; Number of threads — 69; Width — 3¼″; Technique — plain weave
Draft:

```
O|O O O O O O O O O O O O O O O M M O O O O O O O O O O O O O O O    = 34
H|O O O B B B B O O G G O O M M M M M M M M O O G G O O B B B B O O O = 35
                                                                       69
```

COLOR KEY — O = orange flecks; B = bright orange; G = gold; M = medium soft brown.

STRIPS #III AND #IV
Weft — doubled; Number of threads — 45; Width — 2″; Technique — plain weave
Draft:

```
O|O O B B O O M M O O G G O O O O O O O O O    = 22
H|O O B B B O M M M O G G G O Y Y Y Y Y Y O O = 23
                                                45
```

COLOR KEY — O = orange flecks; B = brown (dark); M = medium brown;
G = gold; Y = yellow.

Illustration 252
Belt Purse (2 strips sewn together)
Yarns — Fine rug yarn — wool; rayon (800 yards per pound)
Weft — doubled
Number of threads — 65 (for each section)
Width — completed — 2½″
Technique — plain weave — stripes
Draft:

```
O|B B B B B B M L L L M M P M B B B B B M P M M L L L M B B B B B B    = 32
H|B B B B B B M L L L M M P M B B B B B M B M M L L L M B B B B B B B = 33
                                                                        65
```

COLOR KEY — B = bright, hot pink; M = deep maroon; L = lavender; P = pink.

Illustration 255 is the same as 37r

Illustration 273

3 STRIPS

Yarns — Rug wool; Weft — doubled; Number of threads — STRIP I — 25, STRIP II — 73, STRIP III — 55; Width — STRIP I — ⅞″, STRIP II — 2¾″, STRIP III — 2½″; Dimensions of Hanging — 12½″ × 26″; Technique — plain weave

Drafts:

OUTSIDE STRIPS (I)

O	D D D D D D D S S D D D	= 12
H	D D D D D D D D S S D D D	= 13
		25

2ⁿᵈ FROM ENDS (II)

O	D D K K K K K K K K T T T T T T T T T N N N N N N N N K K K K K
H	D D D D D D D D K K K K K K K K T T T T T T T T T N N N N N N N

(*continued*)

O	K K	= 36
H	N N N	= 37
		73

CENTER SECTIONS (III)

O	K K K K K K K K M M M M M M M M S S S S S S S S L	= 27
H	K K M M M M M M M M S S S S S S S S S L L L L L L L L	= 28
		55

COLOR KEY — D = dark olive; S = spring green; K = kelly green; T = turquoise; N = navy blue; M = medium olive; L = light green.

Illustration 276

HANDLE

Yarn — Acrylic — knitting worsted type — 4 ply flecked and solid colors

Weft — doubled; Number of threads — 59; Width — 2¾″; Technique — plain weave

Draft:

```
O | O O O O O B B B B B B B B B B B B B B B B B B B O O O O O     = 29
H | O O O B B B B O O O O O O O O O O O O O O O O B B B B O O O   = 30
                                                                    59
```

COLOR KEY — O = orange flecked; B = dark brown.

BODY OF PURSE (2 strips)
Yarn — 4 ply, knitting worsted type — orange flecks, and colors as below.
Weft — doubled; Number of threads — 89; Width — 4¼″ (each strip); Technique — plain weave
Draft:

```
O | O O O O O O O O B B O O O O O O O O O O O O O O O O O O O O O O O O O O O
H | O O O O O B B B B B B B B O O O O O O O O P P P P O O L L L L O O G G
```

(*continued*)

```
O | O O O O O O     = 44
H | G O O O O O O = 45
                     89
```

COLOR KEY — O = orange flecked; B = dark brown; P = pale gold; L = pale orange;
G = bright, shiny gold.

Illustration 277
Xmas Runner 2 strips — cut and put together. (Outside strips — same as bell pull)
Yarn — bulky acrylic
Weft — doubled
Number of threads — 188 (2 strips @ 45; 2 strips @ 49)
Width — total — 12½″; Length — 38″ including fringe (longest)
Technique — plain weave — strips designed so that when put together
would give appearance of one wide woven piece.
Draft — OUTSIDE STRIP: *same as 37d*
Draft — MIDDLE STRIPS: (connected by facing each other to widen
appearance of pattern) = *same as 37l*

Suppliers

Table Model Loom

Schacht Spindle Co.
1708 Walnut St.
Boulder, Colo. 80302

Floor and Table Model Looms

The Unicorn
Box 645
Rockville, Md. 20851

Yarns

Local yarn stores, variety stores,
and hobby stores.

Weavers' supply shops.

Craft Yarns of Rhode Island
Main St.
Harrisville, R.I. 02830

Frederick J. Fawcett, Inc.
129 South St.
Boston, Mass. 02111

Greentree Ranch
163 N. Carter Lake Rd.
Loveland, Colo. 80537

Yarns (cont.)

Lily Mills
Box 88
Shelby, N.C. 28150

Robin and Russ
533 N. Adams St.
McMinnville, Oregon 97128

The Unicorn
Box 645
Rockville, Md. 20851

Yarn Depot
545 Sutter St.
San Francisco, Calif. 94102

Bibliography

Atwater, Mary Meigs. *Byways in Handweaving*. New York: The Macmillan Co., 1954

Birrell, Verla. *The Textile Arts*: A Handbook of Fabric Structure and Design Processes: Ancient and Modern Weaving, Braiding and Printing, and Other Textile Techniques. New York: Harper & Brothers, 1959

Bitustol, Torbjorg. *Vava i bandgrind*. Stockholm: LTS forlag, 1968

Merisalo, Viivi, *Nauhoja*. Porvoo, Finland. Werner Soderstrom Osakeyhtio, 1966

Naumann, Rose and Raymond Hull. *The Off-Loom Weaving Book*. New York: Charles Scribner's Sons, 1973

Moseley, Spencer, et al. *Crafts Design: An Illustrated Guide*. Belmont, California: Wadsworth Publishing Co., 1962

Tidball, Harriet Douglas. *The Inkle Weave*. Virginia City, Montana: Shuttle Craft Guild, 1952

Tidball, Harriet D. *Weaving Inkle Bands*. Shuttle Craft Guild Monograph 27. Lansing, Michigan: Shuttle Craft Guild, 1969

Trotzig, Liv and Astrid Axelsson. *Band*. Stockholm: ICA Forlaget, 1958

Trotzig, Liv and Astrid Axelsson. *Band*. Vasteras, Sweden: ICA Forlaget, 1972

West, Virginia M. *Finishing Touches for the Handweaver*. Newton Center, Mass. Charles T. Branford Co. 1968

For Design Ideas

Appleton, LeRoy H. *American Indian Design and Decoration*. New York: Dover Publications, Inc. 1971

Crusch, Put A. *Engadiner Kreuzstichmuster*. Chur, Switzerland: Verlegt Bei Bischofberger & Co. 1969

Hunt, W. Ben and J. F. "Buck" Burshears. *American Indian Beadwork*. New York: Collier Books, 1973

Humbert, Claude, Ed. *Ornamental Design*. New York: Viking Press, 1970

Jornung, Mannt Mule. *Vaevemonstre: for alle slags vaeve*. Denmark: Jul Gjellerups Forlag, 1952

Lyford, Carrie A. *Ojibwa Crafts (Chippewa)*. Lawrence, Kansas: Haskell Press. 1943

Lyford, Carrie A. *Quill and Beadwork of the Western Sioux*. Lawrence, Kansas: Haskell Press, 1940

Editions Th. de Dillmont. *Marking Stitch, 4th Series*. Mulhouse, France:
    Dollfus-Mieg & Cie., n.d.

Editions Th. de Dillmont. *Morocco Embroideries*. Mulhouse, France. Dollfus-
    Mieg & Cie., n.d.

De Neergaard, Helga Bruun. *Avigtat: Gronlandske skindmonstre*. Denmark:
    Host & Sons Forlag, 1962

O'Neale, Lila M. *Textiles of Highland Guatemala*. Washington, D.C. Carnegie
    Institution of Washington, 1945

Punto a Croce, 10th Series. Milan, Italy: S.I.E.S. 1969

Index